THE ROAR
OF THE CROWD

A SPORTING ANTHOLOGY

THE ROAR
OF THE CROWD

A SPORTING ANTHOLOGY

selected by
Julian Walker

THE BRITISH LIBRARY

To Pete, triathlete and Wolves supporter

CONTENTS

6 THE CULTURE OF SPORT

7 LOVE AND HATE

INTRODUCTION

This anthology of sporting literature covers sport in fiction, memoir, reportage, history, satirical poetry, instruction and more. What has governed the selection of the texts is not dissimilar to what governs my interest in sport, as a participant or spectator: these pieces have excited me, caught my eye, made me feel good or just been fun to read. Some of the texts are as familiar as the Grand National; others I came across by chance and, like Alice finding herself suddenly involved in the Queen's croquet match, I was inexorably drawn in. I hope the reader's engagement will similarly range from the counterpart of being on the pitch to craning to watch a cricket match from a train window.

Is it possible to compare the literature of sport with sport itself? A dull match may come to life in the words of a good writer, but we might also ask whether writing can ever equal the thrill of a live match. So is sports-writing a part of sport, or a different thing altogether? Does it take the mind of a writer to give sport meaning?

To answer these questions we may start by considering what sport means. Sport means everything and nothing. The physical and psychological effects can be both beneficial and disastrous. On the physical side we may get stronger, or injured, or more self-aware, or enter some deep bodily calm of concentration or achievement; while on the mental side, nothing can take away the knowledge of victory or of defeat. We know that sporting prowess does not automatically confer bodily health or long life, but we know too that the memory of enjoyment, success or failure can last a lifetime.

This raises the question of the relationship between participating and winning. Many of the texts here celebrate taking part, whether for fun, interest or dedication. For some of the participants it matters, in Grantland Rice's elegant words, 'not that you won or lost, but how you played the game'. Other texts here are about the sacrifice of everything for winning. The culture of sport somehow embraces beach games and the World Cup, the science of health supplements that give the slightest of edges, and the unwritten rules that comprise the 'spirit of the game'. On the difference between winning and losing a complex culture has been built, a culture that both encourages the casual participant and praises the spirit of amateurism, while simultaneously idolising the record-holder and creating a different kind of model for the human frame. This complicated relationship matters because we know that winning and losing are essential factors of sport.

Simon Barnes wrote in *The Meaning of Sport*, 'Perhaps sport matters because it doesn't matter'. My take on this is that because it doesn't matter, sport can be anything we want it to be: partisan-ship, admiration of the human body, a bit of fun, the sublimation of combat, the testing of what we are and what we can be. Sport is the ultimate example of a construct built on the most basic thing we have: our bodies. It is essentially a momentary event made from something that we know cannot last. But what does last is the story. For Richard Holt, in *Sport and the British*, sports have 'a heroic and mythical dimension', while Simon Barnes sees sport as a compli-cated metaphor: tennis as a duel, horse-racing as evolution, cricket as an unfolding image of life and death. If sport is what Clifford Geertz described as 'a story we tell ourselves about ourselves', writing about sport is an attempt to understand the metaphor, the story about the story, which simultaneously embellishes and reveals.

Some of the texts here are light, though not necessarily single-layered; others combine the gravitas of the umpire with the penetration of the fly-half. Ernest Hemingway writing about the relationship between the angler and the fish, or Joyce Carol Oates analysing the essence of boxing, or Alan Sillitoe on the runner's self-awareness and judgment, talk to us directly about the nature of being human. Some of the texts surprise, such as the techniques of nineteenth-century athletics preparation, or a polo match seen from the ponies' point of view. Others gently draw us into the idea of sport as 'deep play': Roger Ascham's allegory of archery and philosophy, John Donne's conceit of love as fishing, George Eliot's delicate irony in her description of the archery club. Also included are some shadow areas: David Storey's portrayal of ambition, or the dark underside of boxing in Ring Lardner's story of destruction.

The various sections look at sport from a range of perspectives, building up to a group of four finalists whose understanding of the subject sees through to its essence. These, for me, show how the best sports-writing can mirror that point where, for the sports fan, cheering is not enough and gives way to wonder.

Julian Walker

I

THE CHALLENGE

It begins long before the starter's gun. There has to be preparation, hunger and will. All of these can be found a thousand years ago in an excerpt from Beowulf, *where Unferth belittles Beowulf and Beowulf comes back at him by bragging over a swimming match.*

The drive, the adrenalin rush, the need to get out there and get stuck in (the subject of the text from Barry Hines's The Blinder*) is shown through the specifics of the body, or bodies together, stressed and desperate to start. Robert Burton and Walter Thom look at the body too − Thom largely concentrating on how the athlete turns food into competitive success, and Burton on the value of exercise to the spirit, bringing in references from a wide range of cultures. In passing, Burton mentions the Roman Stoic philosopher Seneca's injunction that we should 'do something, though it be to no purpose'. Doris Lessing's story is about 'doing something', which must, absolutely, be done, and this gives rise to our first sporting paradox − the before and after of sport. For the boy, once the challenge was met, it 'was no longer of the least importance'.*

The relationship between 'meaning everything' and 'meaning nothing' runs through many of the texts in this collection. C. L. R. James, building a career from watching cricket as well as politics, shows a keen awareness of the wider meaning of sport.

Lest we should think that equipment branding is a thing of modern times, Thomas Mathison's mock-heroic celebration of golf praises an eighteenth-century golf-ball maker whose fame is such that, as he rounds off his working day with a stroll round the streets of St Andrews playing his bagpipes, young men and women leave off their dancing to shout his name. This is the kind of advertising money cannot buy.

DORIS LESSING

Through the Tunnel (1955)

Going to the shore on the first morning of the holiday, the young English boy stopped at a turning of the path and looked down at a wild and rocky bay, and then over to the crowded beach he knew so well from other years. His mother walked on in front of him, carrying a bright striped bag in one hand. Her other arm, swinging loose, was very white in the sun. The boy watched that white, naked arm, and turned his eyes, which had a frown behind them, towards the bay and back again to his mother. When she felt he was not with her, she swung around. 'Oh, there you are, Jerry!' she said. She looked impatient, then smiled. 'Why, darling, would you rather not come with me? Would you rather –' She frowned, conscientiously worrying over what amusements he might secretly be longing for, which she had been too busy or too careless to imagine. He was very familiar with that anxious, apologetic smile. Contrition sent him running after her. And yet, as he ran, he looked back over his shoulder at the wild bay; and all morning, as he played on the safe beach, he was thinking of it.

Next morning, when it was time for the routine of swimming and sunbathing, his mother said, 'Are you tired of the usual beach, Jerry? Would you like to go somewhere else?'

'Oh, no!' he said quickly, smiling at her out of that unfailing impulse of contrition – a sort of chivalry. Yet, walking down the path with her, he blurted out, 'I'd like to go and have a look at those rocks down there.'

She gave the idea her attention. It was a wild-looking place, and there was no one there, but she said, 'Of course, Jerry. When you've had enough, come to the big beach. Or just go straight back to the villa, if you like.' She walked away, that bare arm, now slightly reddened from yesterday's sun, swinging. And he almost ran after her again, feeling it unbearable that she should go by herself, but he did not.

She was thinking, Of course he's old enough to be safe without me. Have I been keeping him too close? He mustn't feel he ought to be with me. I must be careful.

He was an only child, eleven years old. She was a widow. She was determined to be neither possessive nor lacking in devotion. She went worrying off to her beach.

As for Jerry, once he saw that his mother had gained her beach, he began the steep descent to the bay. From where he was, high up among red-brown rocks, it was a scoop of moving bluish green fringed with white. As he went lower, he saw that it spread among small promontories and inlets of rough, sharp rock, and the crisping, lapping surface showed stains of purple and darker blue. Finally, as he ran sliding and scraping down the last few yards, he saw an edge of white surf and the shallow, luminous movement of water over white sand, and, beyond that, a solid heavy blue.

He ran straight into the water and began swimming. He was a good swimmer. He went out fast over the gleaming sand, over a middle region where rocks lay like discoloured monsters under the surface and then he was in the real sea – a warm sea where irregular cold currents from the deep water shocked his limbs.

When he was so far out that he could look back not only on the little bay but past the promontory that was between it and the big beach, he floated on the buoyant surface and looked for his mother. There she was, a speck of yellow under an umbrella that looked like a slice of orange peel. He swam back to shore, relieved at being sure she was there, but all at once very lonely.

On the edge of a small cape that marked the side of the bay away from the promontory was a loose scatter of rocks. Above them, some boys were stripping off their clothes. They came running, naked, down to the rocks. The English boy swam towards them, but kept his distance at a stone's throw. They were of that coast; all of them were burned smooth dark brown and speaking a language he did not understand. To be with them, of them, was a craving that filled his whole body. He swam a little closer; they turned and watched him with narrowed, alert dark eyes. Then one smiled and waved. It was enough. In a minute, he had swum in and was on the rocks beside them, smiling with a desperate, nervous supplication. They shouted cheerful greetings at him; and then, as he preserved his nervous, uncomprehending smile, they understood that he was a foreigner strayed from his own beach, and they proceeded to forget him. But he was happy. He was with them.

They began diving again and again from a high point into a well of blue sea between rough, pointed rocks. After they had dived and come up, they swam around, hauled themselves up, and waited their turn to dive again. They were big boys – men, to Jerry. He dived, and they watched him; and when he swam around to take his place, they made way for him. He felt he was accepted and he dived again, carefully, proud of himself.

Soon the biggest of the boys poised himself, shot down into the water, and did not come up. The others stood about, watching. Jerry, after waiting for the sleek brown head to appear, let out a yell of warning; they looked at him idly and turned their eyes back towards the water. After a long time, the boy came up on the other side of a big dark rock, letting the air out of his lungs in a sputtering gasp and a shout of triumph. Immediately the rest of them dived in. One moment, the morning seemed full of chattering boys; the next, the air and the surface of the water were empty. But through the heavy blue, dark shapes could be seen moving and groping.

Jerry dived, shot past the school of underwater swimmers, saw a black wall of rock looming at him, touched it, and bobbed up at once to the surface, where the wall was a low barrier he could see across. There was no one visible; under him, in the water, the dim shapes of the swimmers had disappeared. Then one, and then another of the boys came up on the far side of the barrier of rock, and he understood that they had swum through some gap or hole in it. He plunged down again. He could see nothing through the stinging salt water but the blank rock. When he came up the boys were all on the diving rock, preparing to attempt the feat again. And now, in a panic of failure, he yelled up, in English, 'Look at me! Look!' and he began splashing and kicking in the water like a foolish dog.

They looked down gravely, frowning. He knew the frown. At moments of failure, when he clowned to claim his mother's attention, it was with just this grave, embarrassed inspection that she rewarded him. Through his hot shame, feeling the pleading grin on his face like a scar that he could never remove, he looked up at the group of big brown boys on the rock and shouted, '*Bonjour! Merci! Au revoir! Monsieur, monsieur!*' while he hooked his fingers round his ears and waggled them.

Water surged into his mouth; he choked, sank, came up. The rock, lately weighted with boys, seemed to rear up out of the water as their weight was removed. They were flying down past him now, into the water; the air was full of falling bodies. Then the rock was empty in the hot sunlight. He counted one, two, three …

At fifty, he was terrified. They must all be drowning beneath him, in the watery caves of the rock At a hundred, he stared around him at the empty hillside, wondering if he should yell for help. He counted faster, faster, to hurry them up, to bring them to the surface quickly, to drown them quickly – anything rather than the terror of counting on and on into the blue emptiness of the morning. And then, at a hundred and sixty, the water beyond the rock was full of boys blowing like brown whales. They swam back to the shore without a look at him.

He climbed back to the diving rock and sat down, feeling the hot roughness of it under his thighs. The boys were gathering up their bits of clothing and running off along the shore to another promontory. They were leaving to get away from him. He cried openly, fists in his eyes. There was no one to see him, and he cried himself out.

It seemed to him that a long time had passed, and he swam out to where he could see his mother. Yes, she was still there, a yellow spot under an orange umbrella. He swam back to the big rock, climbed up, and dived into the blue pool among the fanged and angry boulders. Down he went, until he touched the wall of rock again. But the salt was so painful in his eyes that he could not see.

He came to the surface, swam to shore and went back to the villa to wait for his mother. Soon she walked slowly up the path, swinging her striped bag, the flushed, naked arm dangling beside her. 'I want some swimming goggles,' he panted, defiant and beseeching.

She gave him a patient, inquisitive look as she said casually, 'Well, of course, darling.'

But now, now, now! He must have them this minute, and no other time. He nagged and pestered until she went with him to a shop. As soon as she had bought the goggles, he grabbed them from her hand as if she were going to claim them for herself, and was off, running down the steep path to the bay.

Jerry swam out to the big barrier rock, adjusted the goggles, and dived. The impact of the water broke the rubber-enclosed vacuum, and the goggles came loose. He understood that he must swim down to the base of the rock from the surface of the water. He fixed the goggles tight and firm, filled his lungs, and floated, face down, on the water. Now, he could see. It was as if he had eyes of a different kind – fish eyes that showed everything clear and delicate and wavering in the bright water.

Under him, six or seven feet down, was a floor of perfectly clean, shining white sand, rippled firm and hard by the tides. Two greyish shapes steered there, like long, rounded pieces of wood or slate. They were fish. He saw them nose towards each other, poise motion-less, make a dart forward, swerve off, and come around again. It was like a water dance. A few inches above them the water sparkled as if sequins were dropping through it. Fish again – myriads of minute fish, the length of his fingernail, were drifting through the water, and in a moment he could feel the innumerable tiny touches of them against his limbs. It was like swimming in flaked silver. The great rock the big boys had swum through rose sheer out of the white sand – black, tufted lightly with greenish weed. He could see no gap in it. He swam down to its base.

Again and again he rose, took a big chestful of air, and went down again. Again and again he groped over the surface of the rock, feeling it, almost hugging it in the desperate need to find the entrance. And then, once, while he was clinging to the black wall, his knees came up and he shot his feet out forward and they met no obstacle. He had found the hole.

He gained the surface, clambered about the stones that littered the barrier rock until he found a big one, and, with this in his arms, let himself down over the side of the rock. He dropped, with the weight, straight to the sandy floor. Clinging tight to the anchor of stone, he lay on his side and looked in under the dark shelf at the place where his feet had gone. He could see the hole. It was an irregular, dark gap but he could not see deep into it. He let go of his anchor, clung with his hands to the edges of the hole, and tried to push himself in.

He got his head in, found his shoulders jammed, moved them in sideways, and was inside as far as his waist. He could see nothing ahead. Something soft and clammy touched his mouth; he saw a dark frond moving against the greyish rock, and panic filled him. He thought of octopuses, of clinging weed. He pushed himself out backwards and caught a glimpse, as he retreated, of a harmless tentacle of seaweed drifting in the mouth of the tunnel. But it was enough. He reached the sunlight, swam to shore, and lay on the diving rock. He looked down into the blue well of water. He knew he must find his way through that cave, or hole, or tunnel, and out the other side.

First, he thought, he must learn to control his breathing. He let himself down into the water with another big stone in his arms, so that he could lie effortlessly on the bottom of the sea. He counted. One, two, three. He counted steadily. He could hear the movement of blood in his chest. Fifty-one, fifty-two … His chest was hurting. He let go of the rock and went up into the air. He saw the sun was low. He rushed to the villa and found his mother at her supper. She said only, 'Did you enjoy yourself?' and he said, 'Yes.'

All night the boy dreamed of the water-filled cave in the rock, and as soon as breakfast was over he went to the bay.

That night, his nose bled badly. For hours he had been underwater, learning to hold his breath, and now he felt weak and dizzy. His mother said, 'I shouldn't overdo things, darling, if I were you.'

That day and the next, Jerry exercised his lungs as if everything, the whole of his life, all that he would become, depended upon it. Again his nose bled at night, and his mother insisted on his coming with her the next day. It was a torment to him to waste a day of his careful self-training, but he stayed with her on that other beach, which now seemed a place for small children, a place where his mother might lie safe in the sun. It was not his beach.

He did not ask for permission, on the following day, to go to his beach. He went, before his mother could consider the complicated rights and wrongs of the matter. A day's rest, he discovered, had improved his count by ten. The big boys had made the passage while he counted a hundred and sixty. He had been counting fast, in his fright. Probably now, if he tried, he could get through that long tunnel, but he was not going to try yet. A curious, most unchildlike persistence, a controlled impatience, made him wait. In the meantime, he lay underwater on the white sand, littered now by stones he had brought down from the upper air, and studied the entrance to the tunnel. He knew every jut and corner of it, as far as it was possible to see. It was as if he already felt its sharpness about his shoulders.

He sat by the clock in the villa, when his mother was not near, and checked his time. He was incredulous and then proud to find he could hold his breath without strain for two minutes. The words 'two minutes', authorized by the clock, brought close the adventure that was so necessary to him.

In another four days, his mother said casually one morning, they must go home. On the day before they left, he would do it. He would do it if it killed him, he said defiantly to himself. But two days before they were to leave – a day of triumph when he increased his count by fifteen – his nose bled so badly that he turned dizzy and had to lie limply over the big rock like a bit of seaweed, watching the thick red blood flow on to the rock and trickle slowly down to the sea. He was frightened. Supposing he turned dizzy in the tunnel? Supposing he died there, trapped? Supposing – his head went around, in the hot sun, and he almost gave up. He thought he would return to the house and lie down, and next summer, perhaps, when he had another year's growth in him – *then* he would go through the hole.

But even after he had made the decision, or thought he had, he found himself sitting up on the rock and looking down into the water; and he knew that now, this moment, when his nose had only just stopped bleeding, when his head was still sore and throbbing – this was the moment when he would try. If he did not do it now, he never would. He was trembling with fear that he would not go; and he was trembling with horror at that long, long tunnel under the rock, under the sea. Even in the open sunlight, the barrier rock seemed very wide and very heavy; tons of rock pressed down on where he would go. If he died there, he would lie until one day – perhaps not before next year – those big boys would swim into it and find it blocked.

He put on his goggles, fitted them tight, tested the vacuum. His hands were shaking. Then he chose the biggest stone he could carry and slipped over the edge of the rock until half of him was in the cool, enclosing water and half in the hot sun. He looked up once at the empty sky, filled his lungs once, twice, and then sank fast to the bottom with the stone. He let it go and began to count. He took the edges of the hole in his hands and drew himself into it, wriggling his shoulders in sideways as he remembered he must, kicking himself along with his feet.

Soon he was clear inside. He was in a small rock-bound hole filled with yellowish-grey water. The water was pushing him up against the roof. The roof was sharp and pained his back. He pulled himself along with his hands – fast, fast – and used his legs as levers. His head knocked against something; a sharp pain dizzied him. Fifty, fifty-one, fifty-two ... He was without light, and the water seemed to press upon him with the weight of rock. Seventy-one, seventy-two ... There was no strain on his lungs. He felt like an inflated balloon, his lungs were so light and easy, but his head was pulsing.

He was being continually pressed against the sharp roof, which felt slimy as well as sharp. Again he thought of octopuses, and wondered if the tunnel might be filled with weed that could tangle him. He gave himself a panicky, convulsive kick forward, ducked his head, and swam. His feet and hands moved freely, as if in open water. The hole must have widened out. He thought he must be swimming fast, and he was frightened of banging his head if the tunnel narrowed.

A hundred, a hundred and one ... The water paled. Victory filled him. His lungs were beginning to hurt. A few more strokes and he would be out. He was counting wildly; he said a hundred and fifteen, and then, a long time later, a hundred and fifteen again. The water was a clear jewel-green all around him. Then he saw, above his head, a crack running up through the rock. Sunlight was falling through it, showing the clean, dark rock of the tunnel, a single mussel shell, and darkness ahead.

He was at the end of what he could do. He looked up at the

crack as if it were filled with air and not water, as if he could put his mouth to it and draw in air. A hundred and fifteen, he heard himself say inside his head – but he had said that long ago. He must go on into the blackness ahead, or he would drown. His head was swelling, his lungs cracking. A hundred and fifteen, a hundred and fifteen pounded through his head, and he feebly clutched at rocks in the dark, pulling himself forward, leaving the brief space of sunlit water behind. He felt he was dying. He was no longer quite conscious. He struggled on in the darkness between lapses into unconsciousness. An immense, swelling pain filled his head, and then the darkness cracked with an explosion of green light. His hands, groping forward, met nothing; and his feet, kicking back, propelled him out into the open sea.

He drifted to the surface, his face turned up to the air. He was gasping like a fish. He felt he would sink now and drown; he could not swim the few feet back to the rock. Then he was clutching it and pulling himself up on to it. He lay face down, gasping. He could see nothing but a red-veined, clotted dark. His eyes must have burst, he thought; they were full of blood. He tore off his goggles and a gout of blood went into the sea. His nose was bleeding, and the blood had filled the goggles.

He scooped up handfuls of water from the cool, salty sea, to splash on his face, and did not know whether it was blood or salt water he tasted. After a time, his heart quietened, his eyes cleared, and he sat up. He could see the local boys diving and playing half a mile away. He did not want them. He wanted nothing but to get back home and lie down.

In a short while, Jerry swam to shore and climbed slowly up the path to the villa. He flung himself on his bed and slept, waking at the sound of feet on the path outside. His mother was coming back. He rushed to the bathroom, thinking she must not see his face with bloodstains, or tearstains, on it. He came out of the bathroom and met her as she walked into the villa, smiling, her eyes lighting up.

'Have a nice morning?' she asked, laying her hand on his warm brown shoulder a moment.

'Oh yes, thank you,' he said.

'You look a bit pale.' And then, sharp and anxious, 'How did you bang your head?'

'Oh, just banged it,' he told her.

She looked at him closely. He was strained; his eyes were glazed-looking. She was worried. And then she said to herself, Oh, don't fuss! Nothing can happen. He can swim like a fish.

They sat down to lunch together.

'Mummy,' he said, 'I can stay under water for two minutes – three minutes, at least.' It came bursting out of him.

'Can you, darling?' she said. 'Well, I shouldn't overdo it. I don't think you ought to swim any more today.'

She was ready for a battle of wills, but he gave in at once. It was no longer of the least importance to go to the bay.

WALTER THOM

From *Pedestrianism; or, An Account of the Performances of Celebrated Pedestrians During the Last and Present Century: With a Full Narrative of Captain Barclay's Public and Private Matches* (1813)

The pedestrian who may be supposed in tolerable condition enters upon his training with a regular course of physic, which consists of three dozes. Glauber Salts are generally preferred; and from one ounce and a half to two ounces are taken each time, with an interval of four days between each doze.[1] After having gone through the course of physic, he commences his regular exercise, which is gradually increased as he proceeds in the training. When the object in view is the accomplishment of a pedestrian match, his regular exercise may be from twenty to twenty-four miles a day. He must rise at five in the morning, run half a mile at the top of his speed up-hill, and then walk six miles at a moderate pace, coming in about seven to breakfast, which should consist of beef-steaks or mutton-chops under-done, with stale bread and old beer. After breakfast, he must again walk six miles at a moderate pace, and at twelve lie down in bed without his clothes for half an hour. On getting up, he must walk four miles, and return by four to dinner, which should also be beef-steaks or mutton-chops, with bread and

---

1   It is not so generally known as it ought to be that a salt, introduced into medical practice by Dr George Pearson of London, is as excellent a purge as Glauber's salt, and has none of the nauseous taste which renders that purge so disagreeable to many persons. The *Phosphat of Soda* is very similar to common salt in taste, and may be given in a basin of gruel or broth, in which it will be scarcely perceptible to the palate, and will also agree with the most delicate stomach.

beer as at breakfast. Immediately after dinner, he must resume his exercise by running half a mile at the top of his speed, and walking six miles at a moderate pace. He takes no more exercise for that day, but retires to bed about eight, and next morning proceeds in the same manner.

After having gone on in this regular course for three or four weeks, the pedestrian must take a four-mile sweat, which is produced by running four miles, in flannel, at the top of his speed. Immediately on returning, a hot liquor is prescribed, in order to promote the perspiration, of which he must drink one English pint. It is termed the sweating liquor, and is composed of the following ingredients, viz. one ounce of caraway-seed; half an ounce of coriander-seed; one ounce of root liquorice; and half an ounce of sugar-candy; mixed with two bottles of cyder, and boiled down to one half. He is then put to bed in his flannels, and being covered with six or eight pairs of blankets, and a feather-bed, must remain in this state from twenty-five to thirty minutes, when he is taken out and rubbed perfectly dry. Being then well wrapt in his great coat, he walks out gently for two miles, and returns to breakfast, which, on such occasions, should consist of a roasted fowl. He afterwards proceeds with his usual exercise. These sweats are continued weekly, till within a few days of the performance of the match, or, in other words, he must undergo three or four of these operations. If the stomach of the pedestrian be foul, an emetic or two must be given about a week before the conclusion of the training, and he is now supposed to be in the highest condition.

Besides his usual or regular exercise, a person under training ought to employ himself in the intervals in every kind of exertion which tends to activity, such as cricket, bowls, throwing quoits, &c. that, during the whole day, both body and mind may be constantly occupied.

From the above account of Capt. Barclay's method of training, it will be seen that he commences with the evacuating process, and that three purgative dozes are deemed sufficient to clear any man from the impurities which it is requisite to throw off, preparatory to entering on the course of regimen and exercise. And in this stage of the business, the objects to be attained are the purification of the animal system, and the promotion of the digestive powers.

The diet or regimen is the next point of consideration, and it is very simple. As the intention of the trainer is to preserve the strength of the pedestrian, he must take care to keep him in good condition by nourishing food. Animal diet is alone prescribed, and beef and mutton are preferred. The lean of fat beef cooked in steaks, with very little salt, is the best, and it should be rather under-done than otherwise. Mutton, being reckoned easy of digestion, may be occasionally given to vary the diet and gratify the taste. The legs of fowls are highly esteemed. It is preferable to have the meat broiled, as much of its nutritive qualities is lost by roasting or boiling.[2] Biscuit and stale bread are the only preparations of vegetable matter which are permitted to be give; and every thing inducing flatulency must be carefully avoided. Veal and lamb are never allowed, nor pork, which operates as a laxative on some people; and all fat or greasy substances are prohibited, as they induce bile and consequently injure the stomach. But it has been proved by experience that the lean of meat contains more nourishment than the fat, and in every case the most substantial food is preferable to any other kind.

Vegetables, such as turnips, carrots, or potatoes, are never given, as they are watery, and of difficult digestion. On the same principle, fish must be avoided, and besides, they are not sufficiently nutritious. Neither butter nor cheese is allowed; the one being very

---

2 'It may serve as a preliminary rule, that *fresh meat* is the most wholesome and nourishing. To preserve these qualities, however, it ought to be *dressed* so as to remain tender and juicy; for it is by this means it will be easily digested, and afford most nourishment.' – *Willich on Diet and Regimen*, p. 313

indigestible, and the other apt to turn rancid on the stomach. Eggs are also forbidden, excepting the yolk taken raw in the morning. And it must be remarked that salt, spiceries, and all kinds of seasonings, with the exception of vinegar, are prohibited.

With respect to liquors, they must be always taken cold; and home-brewed beer, old, but not bottled, is the best. A little red wine, however, may be given to those who are not fond of malt liquor; but never more than half a pint after dinner. Too much liquor swells the abdomen, and of course injures the breath. The quantity of beer, therefore, should not exceed three pints during the whole day, and it must be taken with breakfast and dinner, no supper being allowed. Water is never given alone, and ardent spirits are strictly prohibited, however diluted. It is an established rule to avoid liquids as much as possible, and no more liquor of any kind is allowed to be taken than what is merely requisite to quench the thirst. Milk is never allowed, as it curdles on the stomach. Soups are not used;[3] nor is any tiling liquid taken warm, but gruel or broth, to promote the operation of the physic; and the sweating liquor mentioned above. The broth must be cooled in order to take off the fat, when it may be again warmed; or beef tea may be used in the same manner, with little or no salt. In the days between the purges, the pedestrian must be fed as usual, strictly adhering to the nourishing diet by which he is invigorated.

Profuse sweating is resorted to as an expedient for removing the superfluities of flesh and fat. Three or four sweats are generally requisite, and they may be considered the severest part of the process.

---

3 'Broths and soups require little digestion; weaken the stomach, and are attended by all the pernicious effects of other warm and relaxing drinks.' – *Willich on Diet &c.*, p. 304

ROBERT BURTON

From *The Anatomy of Melancholy* (1621)

Exercise rectified of Body and Mind.

To that great inconvenience, which comes on the one side by immoderate and unseasonable exercise, too much solitariness and idleness on the other, must be opposed as an antidote, a moderate and seasonable use of it, and that both of body and mind, as a most material circumstance, much conducing to this cure, and to the general preservation of our health. The heavens themselves run continually round, the sun riseth and sets, the moon increaseth and decreaseth, stars and planets keep their constant motions, the air is still tossed by the winds, the waters ebb and flow to their conservation no doubt, to teach us that we should ever be in action. For which cause Hieron prescribes Rusticus the monk that he be always occupied about some business or other, 'that the devil do not find him idle'. Seneca would have a man do something, though it be to no purpose. Xenophon wisheth one rather to play at tables, dice, or make a jester of himself (though he might be far better employed) than do nothing. The Egyptians of old, and many flourishing commonwealths since, have enjoined labour and exercise to all sorts of men, to be of some vocation and calling, and give an account of their time, to prevent those grievous mischiefs that come by idleness: 'for as fodder, whip, and burthen belong to the ass: so meat, correction, and work unto the servant,' Ecclus. xxxiii. 23. The Turks enjoin all men whatsoever, of what degree, to be of some trade or other, the Grand Signior himself is not excused. 'In our memory' (saith Sabellicus) 'Mahomet the Turk, he that conquered Greece, at that very time when he heard ambassadors of other princes, did either carve or cut wooden spoons, or frame something upon a table.' This present sultan makes notches for bows. The

Jews are most severe in this examination of time. All well-governed places, towns, families, and every discreet person will be a law unto himself. But amongst us the badge of gentry is idleness: to be of no calling, not to labour, for that's derogatory to their birth, to be a mere spectator, a drone, *fruges consumere natus*, to have no necessary employment to busy himself about in church and commonwealth (some few governors exempted), 'but to rise to eat,' &c., to spend his days in hawking, hunting, &c., and such like disports and recreations (which our casuists tax), are the sole exercise almost, and ordinary actions of our nobility, and in which they are too immoderate. And thence it comes to pass, that in city and country so many grievances of body and mind, and this feral disease of melancholy so frequently rageth, and now domineers almost all over Europe amongst our great ones. They know not how to spend their time (disports excepted, which are all their business), what to do, or otherwise how to bestow themselves: like our modern Frenchmen, that had rather lose a pound of blood in a single combat than a drop of sweat in any honest labour. Every man almost hath something or other to employ himself about, some vocation, some trade, but they do all by ministers and servants, *ad otia duntaxat se natos existimant, imo ad sui ipsius plerumque et aliorum perniciem*, as one freely taxeth such kind of men, they are all for pastimes, 'tis all their study, all their invention tends to this alone, to drive away time, as if they were born some of them to no other ends. Therefore to correct and avoid these errors and inconveniences, our divines, physicians, and politicians, so much labour, and so seriously exhort; and for this disease in particular, 'there can be no better cure than continual business,' as Rhasis holds, 'to have some employment or other, which may set their mind awork, and distract their cogitations.' Riches may not easily be had without labour and industry, nor learning without study, neither can our health be preserved without bodily exercise. If it be of the body, Guianerius allows that exercise which is gentle, 'and still after those ordinary frications' which must be used every morning. Montaltus, *cap. 26.* and Jason Pratensis use almost the same words, highly commending exercise if it be moderate; 'a wonderful help so used,' Crato calls it,' and a great means to preserve our health, as adding strength to the whole body, increasing natural heat, by means of which the nutriment is well concocted in the stomach, liver, and veins, few or no crudities left, is happily distributed over all the body.' Besides, it expels excrements by sweat and other insensible vapours; insomuch, that Galen prefers exercise before all physic, rectification of diet, or any regimen in what kind soever; 'tis nature's physician. Fulgentius, out of Gordonius *de conserv. vit. hom. lib. 1. cap. 7.* terms exercise, 'a spur of a dull, sleepy nature, the comforter of the members, cure of infirmity, death of diseases, destruction of all mischiefs and vices.' The fittest time for exercise is a little before dinner, a little before supper, or at any time when the body is empty. Montanus, *consil. 31.* prescribes it every morning to his patient, and that, as Calenus adds, 'after he hath done his ordinary needs, rubbed his body, washed his hands and face, combed his head and gargarised.' What kind of exercise he should use, Galen tells us, *lib. 2. et 3. de sanit. tuend.* and in what measure, 'till the body be ready to sweat,' and roused up; *ad ruborem*, some say, *non ad sudorem*, lest it should dry the body too much; others enjoin those wholesome businesses, as to dig so long in his garden, to hold the plough, and the like. Some prescribe frequent and violent labour and exercises, as sawing every day so long together (*epid. 6.* Hippocrates confounds them), but that is in some cases, to some peculiar men; the most forbid, and by no means will have it go farther than a beginning sweat, as being perilous if it exceed.

Of these labours, exercises, and recreations, which are likewise included, some properly belong to the body, some to the mind, some more easy, some hard, some with delight, some without, some within doors, some natural, some are artificial. Amongst bodily exercises, Galen commends *ludum parvæ pilæ*, to play at ball, be it with the hand or racket, in tennis-courts or otherwise, it exerciseth each part of the body, and doth much good, so that they sweat not too much. It was in great request of old amongst the Greeks, Romans, Barbarians, mentioned by Homer, Herodotus, and Plinius. Some write that Aganella, a fair maid of Corcyra, was the inventor of it, for she presented the first ball that ever was made to Nausica, the daughter of King Alcinous, and taught her how to use it.

C. L. R. JAMES

From *A Majestic Innings* (1986)

Patil's innings was a great one. But that does not make him a great batsman in the historic sense of that noble term. Let me illustrate from a personal experience what the term 'great batsman' means.

Some time in the 1920s, Trinidad was playing against Barbados at the Queens Park Oval in Trinidad. Late in the afternoon of the first day, Challenor and Tarilton opened the innings for Barbados. Now Challenor symbolized batting, in every palace and hovel in the Caribbean. Challenor had made his reputation in England in 1923 as one of the great batsmen of the period. Tarilton was not as brilliant but perhaps more reliable. Challenor and Tarilton greeted all cricket invaders of Barbados with a century each, specializing in inflicting this on the visiting MCC teams. So the famous pair walked to the wicket in the gathering dusk to face the bowling of Aucher Waddell. I knew Waddell's bowling well. He was captain of the club of which I was the vice-captain (he and I opened the bowling; I fielded at second slip).

So, ensconced behind the white board where I could see directly along the line between the wickets, I watched Waddell begin as I had seen him do dozens of times. The first ball was shortish and pitched well outside the off-stump. That was Waddell's way of finding his range, so to speak. The next two balls were on the middle stump, good length and of a fine pace. Challenor played a forward defensive stroke, a stroke of certainty and command. I knew what was coming next. Without change of action, Waddell increased his pace and the ball began outside the leg stump. Challenor put his left foot forward, prepared to glance, and did so. But the new ball swung into the wicket very late, eluding Challenor's bat and hitting him on the pad. There was the usual appeal, not only from

the bowler but from the crowd, and I was in it. But the umpire, Toby Creighton – a very sophisticated young Trinidadian – said no. Some time afterwards I met Toby, with whom I used to talk.

'Hi, Toby,' I said, 'you know that Challenor was out in that first over.'

'I know he was out,' said Toby.

I was dumbstruck. 'You knew at the time that he was out?'

Toby very firmly replied that at the time he knew.

'But if you knew,' I said, 'why didn't you give him out?' Toby replied firmly: 'Give him out? You wanted me to give out Challenor lbw for nought, opening the Barbados innings a few minutes before the close of play? Nello, you surprise me. I thought you had more sense than that. Would you have given him out?'

I found I was unable to answer yes. For the first time, I became aware of the enormous quake that would have shuddered through the body politic of the Caribbean if Challenor, of the world-famous firm of Challenor and Tarilton, had been given out lbw for nought a few minutes before the close of play. To this day, some fifty years afterwards, I have not been able to say: 'Yes, I would have given him out.'

For the first time I recognized what it really means in Terra Britannica to be a great batsman.

THE BEOWULF POET

From *Beowulf*, translated by William Morris (1895)

Spake out then Unferth that bairn was of Ecglaf,
And he sat at the feet of the lord of the Scyldings,
He unbound the battle-rune; was Beowulf's faring,
Of him the proud mere-farer, mickle unliking,
Whereas he begrudg'd it of any man other
That he glories more mighty the middle-garth over
Should hold under heaven than he himself held:
   Art thou that Beowulf who won strife with Breca
On the wide sea contending in swimming,
When ye two for pride's sake search'd out the floods
And for a dolt's cry into deep water
Thrust both your life-days? No man the twain of you,
Lief or loth were he, might lay wyte to stay you
Your sorrowful journey, when on the sea row'd ye;
Then when the ocean-stream ye with your arms deck'd,
Meted the mere-streets, there your hands brandish'd!
O'er the Spearman ye glided; the sea with waves welter'd,
The surge of the winter. Ye twain in the waves' might
For a seven nights swink'd. He outdid thee in swimming,
And the more was his might; but him in the morn-tide
To the Heatho-Remes' land the holm bore ashore.
And thence away sought he to his dear land and lovely,
The lief to his people sought the land of the Brondings,
The fair burg peace-warding, where he the folk owned,
The burg and the gold rings. What to theeward he boasted,
Beanstan's son, for thee soothly he brought it about.
Now ween I for thee things worser than erewhile,

Though thou in the war-race wert everywhere doughty,
In the grim war, if thou herein Grendel darest
Night-long for a while of time nigh to abide.
   Then Beowulf spake out, the Ecgtheow's bairn:
What! thou no few of things, O Unferth my friend,
And thou drunken with beer, about Breca hast spoken,
Saidest out of his journey; so the sooth now I tell:
To wit, that the more might ever I owned,
Hard wearing on wave more than any man else.
We twain then, we quoth it, while yet we were younglings,
And we boasted between us, the twain of us being yet
In our youth-days, that we out onto the Spearman
Our lives would adventure; and e'en so we wrought It.
We had a sword naked, when on the sound row'd we,
Hard in hand, as we twain against the whale-fishes
Had mind to be warding us. No whit from me
In the waves of the sea-flood afar might he float
The hastier in holm, nor would I from him hie me.
Then we two together, we were in the sea
For a five nights, till us twain the flood drave asunder,
The weltering of waves. Then the coldest of weathers
In the dusking of night and the wind from the northward
Battle-grim turn'd against us, rough grown were the billows.
Of the mere-fishes then was the mood all up-stirred;
There me 'gainst the loathly the body-sark mine,
The hard and the hand-lock'd, was framing me help,
My battle-rail braided, it lay on my breast
Gear'd graithly with gold. But me to the ground tugg'd
A foe and fiend-scather; fast he had me In hold
That grim one in grip: yet to me was it given.
That the wretch there, the monster, with point might I reach,
With my bill of the battle, and the war-race off bore
The mighty mere-beast through the hand that was mine.

THOMAS MATHISON

The Goff. An Heroi-comical poem. In Three Cantos. (1743)

Goff, and the Man, I sing, who em'lous plies
The jointed club; whose balls invade the skies;
Who from Edina's tow'rs, his peaceful home,
In quest of fame o'er Letha's plains did roam.
Long toil'd the hero, on the verdant field,
Strain'd his stout arm the weighty club to wield;
Such toils it cost, such labours to obtain
The bays of conquest, and the bowl to gain.

O thou GOLFINIA, Goddess of these plains,
Great patroness of GOFF, indulge my strains;
Whether beneath the thorn-tree shade you lie,
Or from Mercerian tow'rs the game survey,
Or 'round the green the flying ball you chase,
Or make your bed in some hot sandy face;
Leave your lov'e abode, inspire his lays,
Who sings of GOFF, and sings thy fav'rite's praise.

North from Edina eight furlongs and more
Lies that fam'd field, on Fortha's sounding shore.
Here, Caledonian Chiefs for health resort,
Confirm their sinews by the manly sport.
Macd----d and umnatch'd D---ple ply
Their pond'rous weapons, and the green defy;
R--tt-y for skill, and C--fe for strength renown'd,
St--rt and L--sly beat the sandy ground,
And Br--wn and Alst--n, Chiefs well known to fame,

And numbers more the Muse forbears to name.
Gigantic B-gg-r here full oft is seen,
Like huge Behemoth on an Indian green;
His bulk enormous scarce can 'scape the eyes,
Amaz'd spectators wonder how he plies.
Yea here great F---s, patron of the just,
The dread of villains, and the good man's trust,
When spent with toils in serving human kind,
His body recreates, and unbends his mind.

Bright Phoebus now, had measur'd half the day
And warm'd the earth with genial noontide ray;
Forth rush'd Castalio and his daring foe,
Both arm'd with clubs, and eager for the blow.
Of finest ash Castalio's shaft was made,
Pond'rous with lead, and fenc'd with horn the head,
(The work of Dickson, who in Letha dwells,
And in the art of making clubs excels),
Which late beneath great Claro's arm did bend,
But now is wielded by his greater friend.

...

The work of Bobson; who with matchless art
Shapes the firm hide, connecting evr'y part,
Then in a socket sets the well-stitch'd void,
And thro' the eylet drives the downy hide;
Crowds urging Crowds the forceful brogue impels,
The feathers harden and the Leather swells;
He crams and sweats, yet crams and urges more,
Till scarce the turgid globe contains its store:
The dreaded falcon's pride here blended lies
With pigeons glossy down of various dyes;

The lark's small pinions join the common stock,
And yellow glory of the martial cock.

Soon as Hyperion gilds old Andrea's spires,
From bed the artist to his cell retires;
With bended back, there plies his steely awls,
And shapes, and stuffs, and finishes the balls.
But when the glorious God of day has driv'n
His flaming chariot down the steep of heav'n,
He ends his labour, and with rural strains
Enchants the lovely maids and weary swains:
As thro' the streets the blythsome piper plays,
In antick dance they answer to his lays;
At ev'ry pause the ravish'd crowd acclaim,
And rend the skies with tuneful Bobson's name.
Not more rewarded was old Amphion's song;
That rear'd a town, and this one drags along.
Such is fam'd Bobson, who in Andrea thrives,
And such the balls each vig'rous hero drives.

The heroes of the poem were Duncan Forbes of Culloden (this was three years before the demise of the Jacobite uprising), Dalrymple, Rattray, Crosse, Lesley, Alston and Biggar. Hawkeyes will note the echoes of the Aeneid in the first few lines. The match seems to have taken place at Leith. If my reading is correct it seems that Bobson finished his working day with a stroll round the streets with his bagpipes. I love the idea of the 'lovely maids and weary swains' dancing through the town, occasionally taking a pause to shout the name of a golf-ball maker.

BARRY HINES

From *The Blinder* (1966)

He walked to the ground. The wind was bitter in the shade of the houses, but the sun was warm when he crossed the streets. Knots of people stood around the ground, but it was still early for the crowds, and the turnstiles only clicked spasmodically. A man was displaying rosettes, stuck to a board like painted lettuce leaves.

'Favours! Favours! Don't forget your favours.'

A gang of boys raced past him, waving their scarves and mocking his call. They wore woollen hats with bobbles stuck on top like rosy apples. They stopped and gathered round a programme seller, who at the same time took their money and gave them programmes one-handed. Lennie pushed the door open into the foyer and walked along the corridor. The dressing-room was warm and clean and smelled of disinfectant. The kit was in order round the walls. The big, white shirt numbers read from two to eleven with the goalkeeper's jersey like a green full stop at the end. The massage table down the centre was draped with a clean towel, and bottles of oil were stacked at its head like bottles behind a bar. Lennie walked to number 10 and sat down above his boots. Eddie was cutting bandages into tie-up lengths.

'All right, son?'

'Fine, thanks.'

Geordie Paling and Wilson O'Neil were studying a racing paper. The other players arrived in ones and twos. They took their coats off straight away and stood talking, hands in pockets. Lennie looked at the clock. It was half past two. He took his shirt off the hook and hung his coat in its place. They were all starting to strip now, slowly and easily.

'Anybody want a rub?'

Chris climbed on to the table and lay with his face on his hands. Eddie began to pummel and rub him with oily palms. Chris moaned.

'Oo, stop it I like it, Eddie.'

Lennie sat in his white shorts and stockings and pulled his boots from under the bench. He squeezed the soft, black leather and turned them over. Long studs had been screwed in to grip the soft ground. Clifford Anderson opened the door and banged Pete Fowler standing behind it.

'All right, lads?'

He sat with the players in turn, speaking softly into their ears. Sometimes they laughed together, then he passed on to the next one. Lennie looped the new laces under his boots and tied them on top, on the tongue.

'All right, son?'

'I'm all right.'

'How many times have you been to the lav?'

Lennie looked up and they both smiled.

'Don't worry, son, they all feel the same, it's only the reaction that's different. Listen at Laurie, you'd think he was going to a party. And Chris there, he looks so relaxed you'd think he was getting ready for bed. But it's there inside just the same, they all feel the same.'

He slapped Lennie on the thigh and stood up.

'You'll be all right, son,'

Max was dispensing lotions like a chemist. Eddie was sweating. Clifford Anderson looked at his watch, then up at the clock and walked out. Lennie stood up and banged his feet. He pulled the red shirt over his head and tucked it in.

'Any tie-ups, Eddie?'

'Here, son.'

Lennie tied the strips of bandage high under the knee, then slipped the bows round to the back and turned the stocking tops into slim neat bands. They were nearly all ready now, stretching and bending, and breathing deeply with hands on hips. The toilets were in constant use and could only be flushed every two or three players. Clifford Anderson returned and closed the door. He spoke to Pete Fowler who moved over and stood with his shoulder to it.

'All ready, lads?'

Lennie hooked two fingers into the drum of Vaseline and smeared a thick streak across his eyebrows. He flattened his hair with his hand and sat down. They were all ready now. 'Right, lads. Two points this afternoon will be a good start to the Christmas programme, and I reckon if you all buckle down and give your best, then we can leave this bad spell behind today. But there's only one way to play as a team, all calling, all helping, all the time. I want one hundred per cent effort for ninety minutes. Now is that clear, lads?'

'Right then. You don't need reminding that these are a hard side. They'll go mad for the first ten minutes, so mark tight and play safe till you're planned in. Laurie, stick close and get that arm up when you're jumping, he's a bugger for back heading. Stan, you know who you're playing against?' Stan nodded. 'Hit him early, well out and he'll not want to know. Plenty of calling, and don't swamp Lennie early on. Right, off you go then and enjoy yourselves.'

They shot up like jack-in-the-boxes and fell into line behind Chris. Clifford Anderson handed him a ball. Eddie gave balls to the next three in line. Fowler opened the door and Chris turned before walking in to the corridor.

'All the best, Len.'

2

THE MATCH

We might not like to be reminded that football and trouble go together, but at least this has been acknowledged for some time. *In* The Bewties of the Fute-ball, *it is not clear whether the 'bewties' are suffered by the spectators or by the players, but probably the difference between these roles was less fixed in 1580. Much more genteel is* England, Their England *– a satirical travelogue in which the cricket match is seen as a microcosm of English eccentricity.*

The idea of sport as a metaphor is seen also in the passage from Homer's Iliad, *which includes boxing and wrestling matches. The contests operate as metaphors for the ten-year-long Trojan War. Ajax and Ulysses grasp each other, but neither can overcome the other as they lock together in parity like the two armies.*

While Alice's engagement in the Red Queen's croquet match is well-known, seeing it in a sporting context allows the possibility of unfamiliar readings. She has a mind for fair play, a clear idea of what is expected of her, and a determination to keep hold of her mallet. A different degree of obsession is displayed by Wodehouse's golfer, while quite the opposite is seen in A Match att Stool-Ball, *in which the match is little more than an excuse for a drunken orgy.*

Concanen's A Match at Football *may not be a model for sports journalism, but it certainly catches the excitement of a game. The* Times *report on the exhibition of swimming by* the Ojibbeway Indians *is a good example of how the Victorian public responded to the 'grotesque antics' of foreign athletes, but this was the first public viewing in Europe of what became the front crawl.*

The final story is the tale of a polo match from the point of view of the ponies. Kipling was a keen polo-player, and his knowledge of the game is matched with his extraordinary ability to create voices.

ANONYMOUS

The Bewties of the Fute-ball (c. 1580)

Brissit brawnis and brokin banis,
Stride, discord and waistie wanis.
Crukit in eild syne halt withal,
Thir are the bewties of the fute-ball.

Modern translation

Torn muscles and broken bones,
Strife, discord and impoverished homes.
Stooping in old age then lameness too,
Those are the beauties of football.

A. G. MACDONNELL

From *England, Their England* (1933)

The batsmen came in. The redoubtable Major Hawker, the fast bowler, thrust out his chin and prepared to bowl. In a quarter of an hour he had terrified seven batsmen, clean bowled six of them, and broken a stump. Eleven runs, six wickets, last man two.

After the fall of the sixth wicket there was a slight delay. The new batsman, the local rate-collector, had arrived at the crease and was ready. But nothing happened. Suddenly the large publisher, who was acting as wicket-keeper, called out, 'Hi! Where's Hawker?'

The words galvanized Mr Hodge into portentous activity.

'Quick!' he shouted. 'Hurry, run, for God's sake! Bob, George, Percy, to the Shoes!' and he set off at a sort of gallop towards the inn, followed at intervals by the rest of the side except the pretty youth in the blue jumper, who lay down; the wicket-keeper, who did not move; and Mr Shakespeare Pollock, who had shot off the mark and was well ahead of the field.

But they were all too late, even Mr Pollock. The gallant Major, admitted by Mr Bason through the back door, had already lowered a quart and a half of mild-and-bitter, and his subsequent bowling was perfectly innocuous, consisting, as it did, mainly of slow, gentle full-pitches to leg which the village baker and even, occasionally, the rate-collector hit hard and high into the long grass. The score mounted steadily.

Disaster followed disaster. Mr Pollock, presented with an easy chance of a run-out, instead of lobbing the ball back to the wicket-keeper had another reversion to his college days and flung it with appalling velocity at the unfortunate rate-collector and hit him in the small of the back, shouting triumphantly as he did so, 'Rah, rah, rah!' Mr Livingstone, good club player, missed two easy catches off successive balls. Mr Hodge allowed another easy catch to fall at his feet without attempting to catch it, and explained afterwards that he had been all the time admiring a particularly fine specimen of oak in the squire's garden. He seemed to think that this was a complete justification of his failure to attempt, let alone bring off, the catch. A black spot happened to cross the eye of the ancient umpire just as the baker put all his feet and legs and pads in front of a perfectly straight ball, and, as he plaintively remarked over and over again, he had to give the batsman the benefit of the doubt, hadn't he? It wasn't as if it was his fault that a black spot had crossed his eye just at that moment. And the stout publisher seemed to be suffering from the delusion that the way to make a catch at the wicket was to raise both hands high in the air, utter a piercing yell, and trust to an immense pair of pads to secure the ball. Repeated experiments proved that he was wrong.

The baker lashed away vigorously and the rate-collector dabbed the ball hither and thither until the score – having once been eleven runs for six wickets – was marked up on the board at fifty runs for six wickets. Things were desperate. Twenty to win and five wickets – assuming that the blacksmith's ankle and third-slip's knee-cap would stand the strain – to fall. If the lines on Mr Hodge's face were deep, the lines on the faces of his team when he put himself on to bowl were like plasticine models of the Colorado Canyon. Mr Southcott, without any orders from his captain, discarded his silk sweater from the Rue de la Paix and went away into the deep field, about a hundred and twenty yards from the wicket. His beautifully brushed head was hardly visible above the daisies. The professor of ballistics sighed deeply. Major Hawker grinned a colossal grin, right across his jolly red face, and edged off in the direction of the Shoes. Livingstone, loyal to his captain, crouched alertly. Mr Shakespeare Pollock rushed about enthusiastically. The remainder of the team drooped.

But the remainder of the team was wrong. For a wicket, a crucial wicket, was secured off Mr Hodge's very first ball. It happened like this. Mr Hodge was a poet, and therefore a theorist, and an idealist. If he was to win a victory at anything, he preferred to win by brains and not by muscle. He would far sooner have his best leg-spinner miss the wicket by an eighth of an inch than dismiss a batsman with a fast, clumsy full-toss. Every ball that he bowled had brain behind it, if not exactness of pitch. And it so happened that he had recently watched a county cricket match between Lancashire, a county that he detested in theory, and Worcestershire, a county that he adored in fact. On the one side were factories and the late Mr Jimmy White; on the other, English apples and Mr Stanley Baldwin. And at this particular match, a Worcestershire bowler, by name Root, a deliciously agricultural name, had outed the tough nuts of the County Palatine by placing all his fieldsmen on the leg-side and bowling what are technically known as 'in-swingers'.

Mr Hodge, at heart an agrarian for all his book-learning and his cadences, was determined to do the same. The first part of the performance was easy. He placed all his men upon the leg-side. The second part – the bowling of the 'in-swingers' – was more compli-cated, and Mr Hodge's first ball was a slow long-hop on the off-side. The rate-collector, metaphorically rubbing his eyes, felt that this was too good to be true, and he struck the ball sharply into the untenanted off-side and ambled down the wicket with as near an approach to gaiety as a man can achieve who is cut off by the very nature of his profession from the companionship and goodwill of his fellows. He had hardly gone a yard or two when he was para-lysed by a hideous yell from the long grass into which the ball had vanished, and still more by the sight of Mr Harcourt, who, aroused from a deep slumber amid a comfortable couch of grasses and daisies, sprang to his feet and, pulling himself together with mirac-ulous rapidity after a lightning if somewhat bleary glance round the field, seized the ball and unerringly threw down the wicket. Fifty for seven, last man twenty-two. Twenty to win: four wickets to fall.

Mr Hodge's next ball was his top-spinner, and it would have, or might have, come very quickly off the ground had it ever hit the ground; as it was, one of the short-legs caught it dexterously and threw it back while the umpire signalled a wide. Mr Hodge then tried some more of Mr Root's stuff and was promptly hit for two sixes and a single. This brought the redoubtable baker to the batting end. Six runs to win and four wickets to fall.

Mr Hodge's fifth ball was not a good one, due mainly to the fact that it slipped out of his hand before he was ready, and it went up and came down in a slow, lazy parabola, about seven feet wide of the wicket on the leg-side. The baker had plenty of time to make up his mind. He could either leave it alone and let it count one run as a wide; or he could spring upon it like a panther and, with a terrific six, finish the match sensationally. He could play the part either of a Quintus Fabius Maximus Cunctator, or of a sort of Tarzan. The baker concealed beneath a modest and floury exterior a mounting ambition. Here was his chance to show the village. He chose the sort of Tarzan, sprang like a panther, whirled his bat cyclonically, and missed the ball by about a foot and a half. The wicket-keeping publisher had also had time in which to think and to move, and he also had covered the seven feet. True, his movements were less like the spring of a panther than the sideways waddle of an aldermanic penguin. But nevertheless he got there, and when the ball had passed the flashing blade of the baker, he launched a mighty kick at it − stooping to grab it was out of the question − and by an amazing fluke kicked it on to the wicket. Even the ancient umpire had to give the baker out, for the baker was still lying flat on his face outside the crease.

'I was bowling for that,' observed Mr Hodge modestly, strolling up the pitch.

'I had plenty of time to use my hands,' remarked the wicket-keeper to the world at large, 'but I preferred to kick it.'

Donald was impressed by the extraordinary subtlety of the game.

'The Ojibbeway Indians', *The Times* (1844)

In consequence of the British Swimming Society having promised to award a first-class silver medal to the best swimmer of these celebrated Indians, the swimming baths in High Holborn, kept by Mr Hedgman, were crowded with private visitors and that gentleman's friends. At 12 o'clock, the omnibus, with three of the Indians outside, and the squaws, accompanied by Mr Anderson, arrived, as also Mr Harold Kenworthy, the well-known swimmer. In the rear of the omnibus, in full costume and on horseback, were 'We-nish-ka-wea-bee' (The Flying Gull) and 'Sah-ma' (Tobacco) with Mr Green, their medical adviser, who has attended them since they have been in London, and who, on this occasion, suggested that the temperature of the water should be raised to 85 degrees. The Flying Gull and Tobacco were selected as competitors, the rest of the party being seated to witness the trial of skill, and the squaws being accommodated in an interior room. While the two Indians were divesting themselves of their costume, Mr Kenworthy went through a series of scientific feats, which excited the applause of the Indians and spectators. At a signal, the Indians jumped into the bath, and, on a pistol being discharged, they struck out and swam to the other end, a distance of 130 feet, in less than half a minute. The Flying Gull was the victor by seven feet. They swam back again to the starting place, where The Flying Gull was again the victor. Then they dived from one end of the bath to the other with the rapidity of an arrow, and almost as straight a tension of limb. They afterwards entered the lists with Mr Kenworthy, who is accounted one of the best swimmers in England, and who beat them with the greatest ease. The Indians then remade their toilet, and the whole party were then shown round the extensive establishment, at which

they expressed great wonder. The medal will be presented to The Flying Gull in the course of the week. Mr Hedgman then conducted them to take refreshment in the room with the squaws, and after partaking of wine and biscuits, they returned in the omnibus to the Egyptian Hall in time to resume the exhibition

LEWIS CARROLL

From *Alice's Adventures in Wonderland* (1865)

The Queen's Croquet-Ground

'Get to your places!' shouted the Queen in a voice of thunder, and people began running about in all directions, tumbling up against each other; however, they got settled down in a minute or two, and the game began. Alice thought she had never seen such a curious croquet-ground in her life; it was all ridges and furrows; the balls were live hedgehogs, the mallets live flamingoes, and the soldiers had to double themselves up and to stand on their hands and feet, to make the arches.

The chief difficulty Alice found at first was in managing her flamingo: she succeeded in getting its body tucked away, comfortably enough, under her arm, with its legs hanging down, but generally, just as she had got its neck nicely straightened out, and was going to give the hedgehog a blow with its head, it WOULD twist itself round and look up in her face, with such a puzzled expression that she could not help bursting out laughing: and when she had got its head down, and was going to begin again, it was very provoking to find that the hedgehog had unrolled itself, and was in the act of crawling away: besides all this, there was generally a ridge or furrow in the way wherever she wanted to send the hedgehog to, and, as the doubled-up soldiers were always getting up and walking off to other parts of the ground, Alice soon came to the conclusion that it was a very difficult game indeed.

The players all played at once without waiting for turns, quarrelling all the while, and fighting for the hedgehogs; and in a very short time the Queen was in a furious passion, and went stamping about, and shouting 'Off with his head!' or 'Off with her head!' about once in a minute.

Alice began to feel very uneasy: to be sure, she had not as yet had any dispute with the Queen, but she knew that it might happen any minute, 'and then,' thought she, 'what would become of me? They're dreadfully fond of beheading people here; the great wonder is, that there's any one left alive!'

She was looking about for some way of escape, and wondering whether she could get away without being seen, when she noticed a curious appearance in the air: it puzzled her very much at first, but, after watching it a minute or two, she made it out to be a grin, and she said to herself 'It's the Cheshire Cat: now I shall have some-body to talk to.'

'How are you getting on?' said the Cat, as soon as there was mouth enough for it to speak with.

Alice waited till the eyes appeared, and then nodded. 'It's no use speaking to it,' she thought, 'till its ears have come, or at least one of them.' In another minute the whole head appeared, and then Alice put down her flamingo, and began an account of the game, feeling very glad she had someone to listen to her. The Cat seemed to think that there was enough of it now in sight, and no more of it appeared.

'I don't think they play at all fairly,' Alice began, in rather a complaining tone, 'and they all quarrel so dreadfully one can't hear oneself speak – and they don't seem to have any rules in particular; at least, if there are, nobody attends to them – and you've no idea how confusing it is all the things being alive; for instance, there's the arch I've got to go through next walking about at the other end of the ground – and I should have croqueted the Queen's hedgehog just now, only it ran away when it saw mine coming!'

'How do you like the Queen?' said the Cat in a low voice.

'Not at all,' said Alice: 'she's so extremely –' Just then she noticed that the Queen was close behind her, listening: so she went on, ' – likely to win, that it's hardly worth while finishing the game.'

The Queen smiled and passed on.

'Who ARE you talking to?' said the King, going up to Alice, and looking at the Cat's head with great curiosity.

'It's a friend of mine – a Cheshire Cat,' said Alice: 'allow me to introduce it.'

'I don't like the look of it at all,' said the King: 'however, it may kiss my hand if it likes.'

'I'd rather not,' the Cat remarked.

'Don't be impertinent,' said the King, 'and don't look at me like that!' He got behind Alice as he spoke.

'A cat may look at a king,' said Alice. 'I've read that in some book, but I don't remember where.'

'Well, it must be removed,' said the King very decidedly, and he called the Queen, who was passing at the moment, 'My dear! I wish you would have this cat removed!'

The Queen had only one way of settling all difficulties, great or small. 'Off with his head!' she said, without even looking round.

'I'll fetch the executioner myself,' said the King eagerly, and he hurried off.

Alice thought she might as well go back and see how the game was going on, as she heard the Queen's voice in the distance, screaming with passion. She had already heard her sentence three of the players to be executed for having missed their turns, and she did not like the look of things at all, as the game was in such confusion that she never knew whether it was her turn or not. So she went in search of her hedgehog.

The hedgehog was engaged in a fight with another hedgehog, which seemed to Alice an excellent opportunity for croqueting one of them with the other: the only difficulty was, that her flamingo was gone across to the other side of the garden, where Alice could see it trying in a helpless sort of way to fly up into a tree.

By the time she had caught the flamingo and brought it back, the fight was over, and both the hedgehogs were out of sight: 'but it doesn't matter much,' thought Alice, 'as all the arches are gone from this side of the ground.' So she tucked it away under her arm, that it might not escape again, and went back for a little more conversation with her friend.

THOMAS D'URFEY

A Match att Stool-Ball (1696)

Come all, great, small, short, tall,
  Away to Stoolball;
Down in a Vale on a Summers day,
All the Lads and Lasses met to be Merry,
A match for Kisses at Stoolball play,
  And for Cakes and Ale,
  And Sider and Perry.
Will and *Tom*, *Hall*, *Dick* and *Hugh*,
Kate, *Doll*, *Sue*, *Bess* and *Moll*,
With *Hodge*, and *Briget*, and *James*, and *Nancy*;
But when plump *Siss* got the ball in her Mutton Fist
Once fretted sh'd hit it farther than any;
Running, Haring, Gaping, Staring,
Reaching, Stooping, Hollowing, Whooping;
  Sun a setting,
  All thought fitting,
  By consent to rest 'em;
Hall got *Sue*, and *Doll* got *Hugh*,
All took by turns their Lasses and Buss'd 'em.
Jolly *Ralph* was in with *Peg*,
Tho' freckl'd like a *Turkey* Egg,
And she as right as is my Leg,
Still gave him leave to towze her.
Harry then to *Katy* swore,
Her Duggs were pretty,
Tho' they were all sweaty,
And large as any Cows are.
Tom Melancholy was

With his Lass;
For *Sue* do what e'er he cou'd do,
Wou'd not note him.
Some had told her,
B'ing a soldier
  In a *Party*
  With *Mac-carty*
At the Siege of *Limrick*,
He was wounded in the *Scrotum*.
But the cunning *Philly*
Was more kind to *Willy*,
Who of all their Ally,
Was the ablest Ringer;
He to carry on the Jest,
Begins a Bumper to the best,
And winks at her of all the rest,
And squeez'd her by the Finger.
Then went the Glasses round,
Then went the Lasses down,
Each Lad did his Sweet-heart own,
And on the Grass did fling her.
Come all, great, small, short, tall,
  Away to Stool Ball.

HOMER

From *The Iliad,* translated by Samuel Butler (1898)

Thereon, the son of Peleus, when he had listened to all the thanks of Nestor, went about among the concourse of the Achaeans, and presently offered prizes for skill in the painful art of boxing. He brought out a strong mule, and made it fast in the middle of the crowd – a she-mule never yet broken, but six years old – when it is hardest of all to break them: this was for the victor, and for the vanquished he offered a double cup. Then he stood up and said among the Argives, 'Son of Atreus, and all other Achaeans, I invite our two champion boxers to lay about them lustily and compete for these prizes. He to whom Apollo vouchsafes the greater endurance, and whom the Achaeans acknowledge as victor, shall take the mule back with him to his own tent, while he that is vanquished shall have the double cup.'

As he spoke there stood up a champion both brave and of great stature, a skilful boxer, Epeus, son of Panopeus. He laid his hand on the mule and said, 'Let the man who is to have the cup come hither, for none but myself will take the mule. I am the best boxer of all here present, and none can beat me. Is it not enough that I should fall short of you in actual fighting? Still, no man can be good at everything. I tell you plainly, and it shall come true; if any man will box with me I will bruise his body and break his bones; therefore let his friends stay here in a body and be at hand to take him away when I have done with him.'

They all held their peace, and no man rose save Euryalus son of Mecisteus, who was son of Talaus. Mecisteus went once to Thebes after the fall of Oedipus, to attend his funeral, and he beat all the people of Cadmus. The son of Tydeus was Euryalus's second, cheering him on and hoping heartily that he would win. First he put a waistband round him and then he gave him some well-cut thongs of ox-hide; the two men being now girt went into the middle of the ring, and immediately fell to; heavily indeed did they punish one another and lay about them with their brawny fists. One could hear the horrid crashing of their jaws, and they sweated from every pore of their skin. Presently Epeus came on and gave Euryalus a blow on the jaw as he was looking round; Euryalus could not keep his legs; they gave way under him in a moment and he sprang up with a bound, as a fish leaps into the air near some shore that is all bestrewn with sea-wrack, when Boreas furs the top of the waves, and then falls back into deep water. But noble Epeus caught hold of him and raised him up; his comrades also came round him and led him from the ring, unsteady in his gait, his head hanging on one side, and spitting great clots of gore. They set him down in a swoon and then went to fetch the double cup.

The son of Peleus now brought out the prizes for the third contest and showed them to the Argives. These were for the painful art of wrestling. For the winner there was a great tripod ready for setting upon the fire, and the Achaeans valued it among themselves at twelve oxen. For the loser he brought out a woman skilled in all manner of arts, and they valued her at four oxen. He rose and said among the Argives, 'Stand forward, you who will essay this contest.'

Forthwith uprose great Ajax, the son of Telamon, and crafty Ulysses, full of wiles rose, also. The two girded themselves and went into the middle of the ring. They gripped each other in their strong hands like the rafters which some master-builder frames for the roof of a high house to keep the wind out. Their backbones cracked as they tugged at one another with their mighty arms – and sweat rained from them in torrents. Many a bloody weal sprang up on their sides and shoulders, but they kept on striving with might and main for victory and to win the tripod. Ulysses could not throw Ajax, nor Ajax him; Ulysses was too strong for him; but when the Achaeans began to tire of watching them, Ajax said to

Ulysses, 'Ulysses, noble son of Laertes, you shall either lift me, or I you, and let Jove settle it between us.'

He lifted him from the ground as he spoke, but Ulysses did not forget his cunning. He hit Ajax in the hollow at the back of his knee, so that he could not keep his feet but fell on his back with Ulysses lying upon his chest, and all who saw it marvelled. Then Ulysses in turn lifted Ajax and stirred him a little from the ground but could not lift him right off it, his knee sank under him, and the two fell side by side on the ground and were all begrimed with dust. They now sprang towards one another and were for wrestling yet a third time, but Achilles rose and stayed them. 'Put not each other further,' said he, 'to such cruel suffering; the victory is with both alike, take each of you an equal prize, and let the other Achaeans now compete.'

Thus did he speak and they did even as he had said, and put on their shirts again after wiping the dust from off their bodies.

P. G. WODEHOUSE

From *The Heart of a Goof* (1925)

It was a morning when all nature shouted 'Fore!' The breeze, as it blew gently up from the valley, seemed to bring a message of hope and cheer, whispering of chip-shots holed and brassies landing squarely on the meat. The fairway, as yet unscarred by the irons of a hundred dubs, smiled greenly up at the azure sky; and the sun, peeping above the trees, looked like a giant golfball perfectly lofted by the mashie of some unseen god and about to drop dead by the pin of the eighteenth. It was the day of the opening of the course after the long winter, and a crowd of considerable dimensions had collected at the first tee. Plus fours gleamed in the sunshine, and the air was charged with happy anticipation.

In all that gay throng there was but one sad face. It belonged to the man who was waggling his driver over the new ball perched on its little hill of sand. This man seemed careworn, hopeless. He gazed down the fairway, shifted his feet, waggled, gazed down the fairway again, shifted the dogs once more, and waggled afresh. He waggled as Hamlet might have waggled, moodily, irresolutely. Then, at last, he swung, and, taking from his caddie the niblick which the intelligent lad had been holding in readiness from the moment when he had walked on to the tee, trudged wearily off to play his second.

The Oldest Member, who had been observing the scene with a benevolent eye from his favourite chair on the terrace, sighed.

'Poor Jenkinson,' he said, 'does not improve.'

'No,' agreed his companion, a young man with open features and a handicap of six. 'And yet I happen to know that he has been taking lessons all the winter at one of those indoor places.'

'Futile, quite futile,' said the Sage with a shake of his snowy head.

'There is no wizard living who could make that man go round in an average of sevens. I keep advising him to give up the game.'

'You!' cried the young man, raising a shocked and startled face from the driver with which he was toying. 'You told him to give up golf! Why I thought –'

'I understand and approve of your horror,' said the Oldest Member, gently. 'But you must bear in mind that Jenkinson's is not an ordinary case. You know and I know scores of men who have never broken a hundred and twenty in their lives, and yet contrive to be happy, useful members of society. However badly they may play, they are able to forget. But with Jenkinson it is different. He is not one of those who can take it or leave it alone. His only chance of happiness lies in complete abstinence. Jenkinson is a goof.'

'A what?'

'A goof,' repeated the Sage. 'One of those unfortunate beings who have allowed this noblest of sports to get too great a grip upon them, who have permitted it to eat into their souls, like some malignant growth. The goof, you must understand, is not like you and me. He broods. He becomes morbid. His goofery unfits him for the battles of life. Jenkinson, for example, was once a man with a glowing future in the hay, corn, and feed business, but a constant stream of hooks, tops, and slices gradually made him so diffident and mistrustful of himself, that he let opportunity after opportunity slip, with the result that other, sterner, hay, corn, and feed merchants passed him in the race. Every time he had the chance to carry through some big deal in hay, or to execute some flashing *coup* in corn and feed, the fatal diffidence generated by a hundred rotten rounds would undo him. I understand his bankruptcy may be expected at any moment.'

'My golly!' said the young man, deeply impressed. 'I hope I never become a goof. Do you mean to say there is really no cure except giving up the game?'

MATTHEW CONCANEN

A Match at Football (1720)

While the bold youths arrang' on either hand,
Around the field in decent order stand,
Amid the Throng lame Hobbinol appear'd,
And Wav'd his Cap in order to be heard.
The Green stood silent as the Midnight-Shade,

All tongues but his were still, when thus he said:
'Ye Champions of fair Lusk, and Ye of Soards,
View well this Ball, the present of your lords.
To outward View, three Folds of Bullocks-hide,
With Leathern Thongs fast bound on ev'ry side:
A Mass of finest Hay conceal'd from sight,
Conspire at once, to make it firm and light
At this you'll all contend, this bravely strive,
Alternate thro' the adverse Goal to drive,
Two Gates of Sally bound the Spacious Green,
Here one, and one on yonder Side is seen.
Guard that Ye Men of Soards, Ye others this;
Fame waits the careful, Scandal the remiss.'
He said, and high in Air he flung the Ball;
The Champions Crowd, and anxious wait its fall.

First Felim, caught; he pois'd and felt it soft,
Then whirld it with a sudden stroke aloft.
With Motion smooth and swift he saw it glide.
'Till Dick, who stop'd it on the other side,
A Dextrous Kick, with artful fury, drew;
The light Machine, with force unerring, new

To th'adverse goal where, in the sight of all
The watchful Daniel caught the flying Ball.
He proudly joyful in his Arms embrac'd
The welcome Prize, then ran with eager haste.
With lusty Strides he measur'd half the Plain,
When all his Foes surround and stop the Swain;
They tug, they pull; to his assistance run
The Strong-limb'd Darby and the Nimble John.
Paddy with more than common ardour fir'd,
Out-singl'd Daniel, while the rest retir'd.
At grapp'ling now their mutual Skill they Try;
Now Arm in Arm they lock, and Thigh in Thigh.
Now turn, now twine, now with a furious bound,
Each lifts his fierce Opposer from the ground.
Till FLORA who perceiv'd the dire debate,
Anxious and trembling for her Darling's fate,
Round Daniel's leg (unseen by human Eyes)
Nine Blades of Grass, with artful Texture ties:
From what slight causes rise our Joy or Grief,
Pleasure or Pain. Affliction or Relief?
Th' entangled Youth, but faintly seems to stand.
Bound by one Leg, Incumber'd in one hand;
For yet be held, nor till his hapless fall
Dropt from his Arms, the long contended Ball.

As when a Mountain Oak its ruin finds,
Which long had brav'd the fury of the Winds,
In vain it stands against the dreadful blast,
And, tho' reluctant, must submit at last,
Such Daniel was thy fall, nor can it be,
To thy reproach, since by the Gods decree.

RUDYARD KIPLING

From *The Maltese Cat* (1936)

They had good reason to be proud, and better reason to be afraid, all twelve of them; for though they had fought their way, game by game, up the teams entered for the polo tournament, they were meeting the Archangels that afternoon in the final match; and the Archangels men were playing with half a dozen ponies apiece. As the game was divided into six quarters of eight minutes each, that meant a fresh pony after every halt. The Skidars' team, even supposing there were no accidents, could only supply one pony for every other change; and two to one is heavy odds. Again, as Shiraz, the grey Syrian, pointed out, they were meeting the pink and pick of the polo-ponies of Upper India, ponies that had cost from a thousand rupees each, while they themselves were a cheap lot gathered, often from country-carts, by their masters, who belonged to a poor but honest native infantry regiment.

'Money means pace and weight,' said Shiraz, rubbing his black-silk nose dolefully along his neat-fitting boot, 'and by the maxims of the game as I know it – '

'Ah, but we aren't playing the maxims,' said The Maltese Cat. 'We're playing the game; and we've the great advantage of knowing the game. Just think a stride, Shiraz! We've pulled up from bottom to second place in two weeks against all those fellows on the ground here. That's because we play with our heads as well as our feet.'

'It makes me feel undersized and unhappy all the same,' said Kittiwynk, a mouse-coloured mare with a red brow-band and the cleanest pair of legs that ever an aged pony owned. 'They've twice our style, these others.'

Kittiwynk looked at the gathering and sighed. The hard, dusty polo-ground was lined with thousands of soldiers, black and white, not counting hundreds and hundreds of carriages and drags and dogcarts, and ladies with brilliant-coloured parasols, and officers in uniform and out of it, and crowds of natives behind them; and orderlies on camels, who had halted to watch the game instead of carrying letters up and down the station; and native horse-dealers running about on thin-eared Biluchi mares, looking for a chance to sell a few first-class polo-ponies. Then there were the ponies of thirty teams that had entered for the Upper India Free-for-All Cup – nearly every pony of worth and dignity, from Mhow to Peshawar, from Allahabad to Multan; prize ponies, Arabs, Syrian, Barb, country-bred, Deccanee, Waziri, and Kabul ponies of every colour and shape and temper that you could imagine. Some of them were in mat-roofed stables, close to the polo-ground, but most were under saddle, while their masters, who had been defeated in the earlier games, trotted in and out and told the world exactly how the game should be played.

It was a glorious sight, and the come and go of the little, quick hooves, and the incessant salutations of ponies that had met before on other polo-grounds or race-courses, were enough to drive a four-footed thing wild.

But the Skidars' team were careful not to know their neighbours, though half the ponies on the ground were anxious to scrape acquaintance with the little fellows that had come from the North, and, so far, had swept the board.

'Let's see,' said a soft gold-coloured Arab, who had been playing very badly the day before, to The Maltese Cat; 'didn't we meet in Abdul Rahman's stable in Bombay, four seasons ago? I won the Paikpattan Cup next season, you may remember?'

'Not me,' said The Maltese Cat, politely. 'I was at Malta then, pulling a vegetable-cart. I don't race. I play the game.'

'Oh!' said the Arab, cocking his tail and swaggering off.

'Keep yourselves to yourselves,' said The Maltese Cat to his companions. 'We don't want to rub noses with all those goose-rumped half-breeds of Upper India. When we've won this Cup they'll give their shoes to know us.'

'We sha'n't win the Cup,' said Shiraz. 'How do you feel?'

'Stale as last night's feed when a muskrat has run over it,' said Polaris, a rather heavy-shouldered grey; and the rest of the team agreed with him.

'The sooner you forget that the better,' said The Maltese Cat, cheerfully. 'They've finished tiffin in the big tent. We shall be wanted now. If your saddles are not comfy, kick. If your bits aren't easy, rear, and let the saises know whether your boots are tight.'

Each pony had his sais, his groom, who lived and ate and slept with the animal, and had betted a good deal more than he could afford on the result of the game. There was no chance of anything going wrong, but to make sure, each sais was shampooing the legs of his pony to the last minute. Behind the saises sat as many of the Skidars' regiment as had leave to attend the match – about half the native officers, and a hundred or two dark, black-bearded men with the regimental pipers nervously fingering the big, beribboned bagpipes. The Skidars were what they call a Pioneer regiment, and the bagpipes made the national music of half their men. The native officers held bundles of polo-sticks, long cane-handled mallets, and as the grand stand filled after lunch they arranged themselves by ones and twos at different points round the ground, so that if a stick were broken the player would not have far to ride for a new one. An impatient British Cavalry Band struck up 'If you want to know the time, ask a p'leeceman!' and the two umpires in light dust-coats danced out on two little excited ponies. The four players of the Archangels' team followed, and the sight of their beautiful mounts made Shiraz groan again.

'Wait till we know,' said The Maltese Cat. 'Two of 'em are playing in blinkers, and that means they can't see to get out of the way of their own side, or they may shy at the umpires' ponies. They've all got white web-reins that are sure to stretch or slip!'

'And,' said Kittiwynk, dancing to take the stiffness out of her, 'they carry their whips in their hands instead of on their wrists. Hah!'

'True enough. No man can manage his stick and his reins and his whip that way,' said The Maltese Cat. 'I've fallen over every square yard of the Malta ground, and I ought to know.'

He quivered his little, flea-bitten withers just to show how satisfied he felt; but his heart was not so light. Ever since he had drifted into India on a troop-ship, taken, with an old rifle, as part payment for a racing debt, The Maltese Cat had played and preached polo to the Skidars' team on the Skidars' stony pologround. Now a polo-pony is like a poet. If he is born with a love for the game, he can be made. The Maltese Cat knew that bamboos grew solely in order that poloballs might be turned from their roots, that grain was given to ponies to keep them in hard condition, and that ponies were shod to prevent them slipping on a turn. But, besides all these things, he knew every trick and device of the finest game in the world, and for two seasons had been teaching the others all he knew or guessed.

'Remember,' he said for the hundredth time, as the riders came up, 'you must play together, and you must play with your heads. Whatever happens, follow the ball. Who goes out first?'

Kittiwynk, Shiraz, Polaris, and a short high little bay fellow with tremendous hocks and no withers worth speaking of (he was called Corks) were being girthed up, and the soldiers in the background stared with all their eyes.

'I want you men to keep quiet,' said Lutyens, the captain of the team, 'and especially not to blow your pipes.'

'Not if we win, Captain Sahib?' asked the piper.

'If we win you can do what you please,' said Lutyens, with a smile, as he slipped the loop of his stick over his wrist, and wheeled to canter to his place. The Archangels' ponies were a little bit above themselves on account of the many-coloured crowd so close to the ground. Their riders were excellent players, but they were a team

W. S. V. Allen
Hampstead.

of crack players instead of a crack team; and that made all the difference in the world. They honestly meant to play together, but it is very hard for four men, each the best of the team he is picked from, to remember that in polo no brilliancy in hitting or riding makes up for playing alone. Their captain shouted his orders to them by name, and it is a curious thing that if you call his name aloud in public after an Englishman you make him hot and fretty. Lutyens said nothing to his men, because it had all been said before.

He pulled up Shiraz, for he was playing 'back,' to guard the goal. Powell on Polaris was half-back, and Macnamara and Hughes on Corks and Kittiwynk were forwards. The tough, bamboo ball was set in the middle of the ground, one hundred and fifty yards from the ends, and Hughes crossed sticks, heads up, with the Captain of the Archangels, who saw fit to play forward; that is a place from which you cannot easily control your team. The little click as the cane-shafts met was heard all over the ground, and then Hughes made some sort of quick wrist-stroke that just dribbled the ball a few yards. Kittiwynk knew that stroke of old, and followed as a cat follows a mouse. While the Captain of the Archangels was wrenching his pony round, Hughes struck with all his strength, and next instant Kittiwynk was away, Corks following close behind her, their little feet pattering like raindrops on glass.

'Pull out to the left,' said Kittiwynk between her teeth; 'it's coming your way, Corks!'

The back and half-back of the Archangels were tearing down on her just as she was within reach of the ball. Hughes leaned forward with a loose rein, and cut it away to the left almost under Kittiwynk's foot, and it hopped and skipped off to Corks, who saw that, if he was not quick, it would run beyond the boundaries. That long bouncing drive gave the Archangels time to wheel and send three men across the ground to head off Corks. Kittiwynk stayed where she was; for she knew the game. Corks was on the ball half a fraction of a second before the others came up, and Macnamara, with a backhanded stroke, sent it back across the ground to Hughes, who saw the way clear to the Archangels' goal, and smacked the ball in before any one quite knew what had happened.

'That's luck,' said Corks, as they changed ends. 'A goal in three minutes for three hits, and no riding to speak of.'

"Don't know,' said Polaris. 'We've made 'em angry too soon. Shouldn't wonder if they tried to rush us off our feet next time.'

'Keep the ball hanging, then,' said Shiraz. 'That wears out every pony that is not used to it.'

Next time there was no easy galloping across the ground. All the Archangels closed up as one man, but there they stayed, for Corks, Kittiwynk, and Polaris were somewhere on the top of the ball, marking time among the rattling sticks, while Shiraz circled about outside, waiting for a chance. 'We can do this all day,' said Polaris, ramming his quarters into the side of another pony. 'Where do you think you're shoving to?'

'I'll – I'll be driven in an ekka if I know,' was the gasping reply, 'and I'd give a week's feed to get my blinkers off. I can't see anything.'

'The dust is rather bad. Whew! That was one for my off-hock. Where's the ball, Corks?'

'Under my tail. At least, the man's looking for it there! This is beautiful. They can't use their sticks, and it's driving 'em wild. Give old Blinkers a push and then he'll go over.'

'Here, don't touch me! I can't see. I'll – I'll back out, I think,' said the pony in blinkers, who knew that if you can't see all round your head, you cannot prop yourself against the shock.

Corks was watching the ball where it lay in the dust, close to his near fore-leg, with Macnamara's shortened stick tap-tapping it from time to time. Kittiwynk was edging her way out of the scrimmage, whisking her stump of a tail with nervous excitement.

'Ho! They've got it,' she snorted. 'Let me out!' and she galloped like a rifle-bullet just behind a tall lanky pony of the Archangels, whose rider was swinging up his stick for a stroke.

'Not today, thank you,' said Hughes, as the blow slid off his raised stick, and Kittiwynk laid her shoulder to the tall pony's quarters, and shoved him aside just as Lutyens on Shiraz sent the ball where it had come from, and the tall pony went skating and slipping away to the left. Kittiwynk, seeing that Polaris had joined Corks in the chase for the ball up the ground, dropped into Polaris' place, and then 'time' was called.

The Skidars' ponies wasted no time in kicking or fuming. They knew that each minute's rest meant so much gain, and trotted off to the rails, and their saises began to scrape and blanket and rub them at once.

'Whew!' said Corks, stiffening up to get all the tickle of the big vulcanite scraper. 'If we were playing pony for pony, we would bend those Archangels double in half an hour. But they'll bring up fresh ones and fresh ones and fresh ones after that – you see.'

'Who cares?' said Polaris. 'We've drawn first blood. Is my hock swelling?'

'Looks puffy,' said Corks. 'You must have had rather a wipe. Don't let it stiffen. You 'll be wanted again in half an hour.'

'What's the game like?' said The Maltese Cat.

"Ground's like your shoe, except where they put too much water on it,' said Kittiwynk. 'Then it's slippery. Don't play in the centre. There's a bog there. I don't know how their next four are going to behave, but we kept the ball hanging, and made 'em lather for nothing. Who goes out? Two Arabs and a couple of country-breds! That's bad. What a comfort it is to wash your mouth out!'

Kitty was talking with a neck of a lather-covered soda-water bottle between her teeth, and trying to look over her withers at the same time. This gave her a very coquettish air.

'What's bad?' said Grey Dawn, giving to the girth and admiring his well-set shoulders.

'You Arabs can't gallop fast enough to keep yourselves warm – that's what Kitty means,' said Polaris, limping to show that his hock needed attention. 'Are you playing back, Grey Dawn?'

"Looks like it,' said Grey Dawn, as Lutyens swung himself up. Powell mounted The Rabbit, a plain bay country-bred much like Corks, but with mulish ears. Macnamara took Faiz-Ullah, a handy, short-backed little red Arab with a long tail, and Hughes mounted Benami, an old and sullen brown beast, who stood over in front more than a polo-pony should.

'Benami looks like business,' said Shiraz. 'How's your temper,

Ben?' The old campaigner hobbled off without answering, and The Maltese Cat looked at the new Archangel ponies prancing about on the ground. They were four beautiful blacks, and they saddled big enough and strong enough to eat the Skidars' team and gallop away with the meal inside them.

'Blinkers again,' said The Maltese Cat. 'Good enough!'

'They're chargers – cavalry chargers!' said Kittiwynk, indignantly. 'They'll never see thirteen-three again.'

'They've all been fairly measured, and they've all got their certificates,' said The Maltese Cat, 'or they wouldn't be here. We must take things as they come along, and keep your eyes on the ball.'

The game began, but this time the Skidars were penned to their own end of the ground, and the watching ponies did not approve of that.

'Faiz-Ullah is shirking – as usual,' said Polaris, with a scornful grunt.

'Faiz-Ullah is eating whip,' said Corks. They could hear the leather-thonged polo-quirt lacing the little fellow's well-rounded barrel. Then The Rabbit's shrill neigh came across the ground.

'I can't do all the work,' he cried, desperately.

'Play the game – don't talk,' The Maltese Cat whickered; and all the ponies wriggled with excitement, and the soldiers and the grooms gripped the railings and shouted. A black pony with blinkers had singled out old Benami, and was interfering with him in every possible way. They could see Benami shaking his head up and down, and flapping his under lip.

'There'll be a fall in a minute, ' said Polaris. 'Benami is getting stuffy.'

The game flickered up and down between goal-post and goal-post, and the black ponies were getting more confident as they felt they had the legs of the others. The ball was hit out of a little scrimmage, and Benami and The Rabbit followed it, Faiz-Ullah only too glad to be quiet for an instant.

The blinkered black pony came up like a hawk, with two of his own side behind him, and Benami's eye glittered as he raced. The question was which pony should make way for the other, for each rider was perfectly willing to risk a fall in a good cause. The black, who had been driven nearly crazy by his blinkers, trusted to his weight and his temper; but Benami knew how to apply his weight and how to keep his temper. They met, and there was a cloud of dust. The black was lying on his side, all the breath knocked out of his body. The Rabbit was a hundred yards up the ground with the ball, and Benami was sitting down. He had slid nearly ten yards on his tail, but he had had his revenge, and sat cracking his nostrils till the black pony rose.

'That's what you get for interfering. Do you want any more?' said Benami, and he plunged into the game. Nothing was done that quarter, because Faiz-Ullah would not gallop, though Macnamara beat him whenever he could spare a second. The fall of the black pony had impressed his companions tremendously, and so the Archangels could not profit by Faiz-Ullah's bad behaviour.

But as The Maltese Cat said when 'time' was called, and the four came back blowing and dripping, Faiz-Ullah ought to have been kicked all round Umballa. If he did not behave better next time The Maltese Cat promised to pull out his Arab tail by the roots and – eat it.

There was no time to talk, for the third four were ordered out.

The third quarter of a game is generally the hottest, for each side thinks that the others must be pumped; and most of the winning play in a game is made about that time.

Lutyens took over The Maltese Cat with a pat and a hug, for Lutyens valued him more than anything else in the world; Powell had Shikast, a little grey rat with no pedigree and no manners outside polo; Macnamara mounted Bamboo, the largest of the team; and Hughes Who's Who, alias The Animal. He was supposed to have Australian blood in his veins, but he looked like a clothes-horse, and

you could whack his legs with an iron crow-bar without hurting him.

They went out to meet the very flower of the Archangels' team; and when Who's Who saw their elegantly booted legs and their beautiful satin skins, he grinned a grin through his light, well-worn bridle.

'My word!' said Who's Who. 'We must give 'em a little football. These gentlemen need a rubbing down.'

'No biting,' said The Maltese Cat, warningly; for once or twice in his career Who's Who had been known to forget himself in that way.

'Who said anything about biting? I'm not playing tiddly-winks. I'm playing the game.' The Archangels came down like a wolf on the fold, for they were tired of football, and they wanted polo. They got it more and more. Just after the game began, Lutyens hit a ball that was coming towards him rapidly, and it rolled in the air, as a ball sometimes will, with the whirl of a frightened partridge. Shikast heard, but could not see it for the minute, though he looked everywhere and up into the air as The Maltese Cat had taught him. When he saw it ahead and overhead he went forward with Powell as fast as he could put foot to ground. It was then that Powell, a quiet and level-headed man, as a rule, became inspired, and played a stroke that sometimes comes off successfully after long practice. He took his stick in both hands, and, standing up in his stirrups, swiped at the ball in the air, Munipore fashion. There was one second of paralysed astonishment, and then all four sides of the ground went up in a yell of applause and delight as the ball flew true (you could see the amazed Archangels ducking in their saddles to dodge the line of flight, and looking at it with open mouths), and the regimental pipes of the Skidars squealed from the railings as long as the pipers had breath. Shikast heard the stroke; but he heard the head of the stick fly off at the same time. Nine hundred and ninety-nine ponies out of a thousand would have gone tearing on after the ball with a useless player pulling at their heads; but Powell knew him, and he knew Powell; and the instant he felt Powell's right leg shift a trifle on the saddle-flap, he headed to the boundary, where a native officer was frantically waving a new stick. Before the shouts had ended, Powell was armed again.

Once before in his life The Maltese Cat had heard that very same stroke played off his own back, and had profited by the confusion it wrought. This time he acted on experience, and leaving Bamboo to guard the goal in case of accidents, came through the others like a flash, head and tail low – Lutyens standing up to ease him – and swept on and on before the other side knew what was the matter, nearly pitching on his head between the Archangels' goal-post as Lutyens kicked the ball in after a straight scurry of a hundred and fifty yards. If there was one thing more than another upon which The Maltese Cat prided himself, it was on this quick, streaking kind of run half across the ground. He did not believe in taking balls round the field unless you were clearly overmatched. After this they gave the Archangels five-minuted football; and an expensive fast pony hates football because it rumples his temper. Who's Who showed himself even better than Polaris in this game. He did not permit any wriggling away, but bored joyfully into the scrimmage as if he had his nose in a feed-box and was looking for something nice. Little Shikast jumped on the ball the minute it got clear, and every time an Archangel pony followed it, he found Shikast standing over it, asking what was the matter.

'If we can live through this quarter,' said The Maltese Cat, 'I sha'n't care. Don't take it out of yourselves. Let them do the lathering.'

So the ponies, as their riders explained afterwards, 'shut-up.' The Archangels kept them tied fast in front of their goal, but it cost the Archangels' ponies all that was left of their tempers; and ponies began to kick, and men began to repeat compliments, and they chopped at the legs of Who's Who, and he set his teeth and stayed where he was, and the dust stood up like a tree over the scrimmage until that hot quarter ended.

They found the ponies very excited and confident when they went to their saises; and The Maltese Cat had to warn them that the worst of the game was coming.

'Now we are all going in for the second time,' said he, 'and they are trotting out fresh ponies. You think you can gallop, but you'll find you can't; and then you'll be sorry.'

'But two goals to nothing is a halter-long lead,' said Kittiwynk, prancing.

'How long does it take to get a goal?' The Maltese Cat answered. 'For pity's sake, don't run away with a notion that the game is half-won just because we happen to be in luck now! They'll ride you into the grandstand, if they can; you must not give 'em a chance. Follow the ball.'

'Football, as usual?' said Polaris. 'My hock's half as big as a nose-bag.'

'Don't let them have a look at the ball, if you can help it. Now leave me alone. I must get all the rest I can before the last quarter.'

He hung down his head and let all his muscles go slack, Shikast, Bamboo, and Who's Who copying his example.

'Better not watch the game,' he said. 'We aren't playing, and we shall only take it out of ourselves if we grow anxious. Look at the ground and pretend it's fly-time.'

They did their best, but it was hard advice to follow. The hooves were drumming and the sticks were rattling all up and down the ground, and yells of applause from the English troops told that the Archangels were pressing the Skidars hard. The native soldiers behind the ponies groaned and grunted, and said things in undertones, and presently they heard a long-drawn shout and a clatter of hurrahs!

'One to the Archangels,' said Shikast, without raising his head. 'Time's nearly up. Oh, my sire and dam!'

'Faiz-Ullah,' said The Maltese Cat, 'if you don't play to the last nail in your shoes this time, I'll kick you on the ground before all the other ponies.'

'I'll do my best when my time comes,' said the little Arab, sturdily.

The saises looked at each other gravely as they rubbed their ponies' legs. This was the time when long purses began to tell, and everybody knew it. Kittiwynk and the others came back, the sweat dripping over their hooves and their tails telling sad stories.

'They're better than we are,' said Shiraz. 'I knew how it would be.'

'Shut your big head,' said The Maltese Cat; 'we've one goal to the good yet.'

'Yes; but it's two Arabs and two country-breds to play now,' said Corks. 'Faiz-Ullah, remember!' He spoke in a biting voice.

As Lutyens mounted Grey Dawn he looked at his men, and they did not look pretty. They were covered with dust and sweat in streaks. Their yellow boots were almost black, their wrists were red and lumpy, and their eyes seemed two inches deep in their heads; but the expression in the eyes was satisfactory.

'Did you take anything at tiffin?' said Lutyens; and the team shook their heads. They were too dry to talk.

'All right. The Archangels did. They are worse pumped than we are.'

'They've got the better ponies,' said Powell. 'I sha'n't be sorry when this business is over.'

That fifth quarter was a painful one in every way. Faiz-Ullah played like a little red demon, and The Rabbit seemed to be every-where at once, and Benami rode straight at anything and everything that came in his way; while the umpires on their ponies wheeled like gulls outside the shifting game. But the Archangels had the better mounts – they had kept their racers till late in the game – and never allowed the Skidars to play football. They hit the ball up and down the width of the ground till Benami and the rest were outpaced. Then they went forward, and time and again Lutyens and Grey Dawn were just, and only just, able to send the ball away with a long, spitting backhander. Grey Dawn forgot that he was an Arab;

and turned from grey to blue as he galloped. Indeed, he forgot too well, for he did not keep his eyes on the ground as an Arab should, but stuck out his nose and scuttled for the dear honour of the game. They had watered the ground once or twice between the quarters, and a careless waterman had emptied the last of his skinful all in one place near the Skidars' goal. It was close to the end of the play, and for the tenth time Grey Dawn was bolting after the ball, when his near hind-foot slipped on the greasy mud, and he rolled over and over, pitching Lutyens just clear of the goal-post; and the triumphant Archangels made their goal. Then 'time' was called – two goals all; but Lutyens had to be helped up, and Grey Dawn rose with his near hind-leg strained somewhere.

'What's the damage?' said Powell, his arm around Lutyens.

'Collar-bone, of course,' said Lutyens, between his teeth. It was the third time he had broken it in two years, and it hurt him.

Powell and the others whistled.

'Game's up,' said Hughes.

'Hold on. We've five good minutes yet, and it isn't my right hand. We'll stick it out.'

'I say,' said the Captain of the Archangels, trotting up, 'are you hurt, Lutyens? We'll wait if you care to put in a substitute. I wish – I mean – the fact is, you fellows deserve this game if any team does. 'Wish we could give you a man, or some of our ponies – or something.'

'You're awfully good, but we'll play it to a finish, I think.'

The Captain of the Archangels stared for a little. 'That's not half bad,' he said, and went back to his own side, while Lutyens borrowed a scarf from one of his native officers and made a sling of it. Then an Archangel galloped up with a big bath-sponge, and advised Lutyens to put it under his armpit to ease his shoulder, and between them they tied up his left arm scientifically; and one of the native officers leaped forward with four long glasses that fizzed and bubbled.

The team looked at Lutyens piteously, and he nodded. It was the last quarter, and nothing would matter after that. They drank out the dark golden drink, and wiped their moustaches, and things looked more hopeful.

The Maltese Cat had put his nose into the front of Lutyens' shirt and was trying to say how sorry he was.

'He knows,' said Lutyens, proudly. 'The beggar knows. I've played him without a bridle before now – for fun.'

'It's no fun now,' said Powell. 'But we haven't a decent substitute.'

'No,' said Lutyens. 'It's the last quarter, and we've got to make our goal and win. I'll trust The Cat.'

'If you fall this time, you'll suffer a little,' said Macnamara.

'I'll trust The Cat,' said Lutyens.

'You hear that?' said The Maltese Cat, proudly, to the others. 'It's worth while playing polo for ten years to have that said of you. Now then, my sons, come along. We'll kick up a little bit, just to show the Archangels this team haven't suffered.'

3

THE VANQUISHED

In a contest between clichés, winning and losing are pretty evenly matched. The winner takes it all, but the race is not always to the swift. What matters is taking part, and winning isn't everything. Except that ultimately, it is. It is hard to take anything from defeat, except the determination to never let it happen again.

Losing is the obvious downside of sport. We are beaten, we lose points, games, matches, championships. We are overcome, lapped, slammed, swept aside, knocked out, thrashed and humiliated. For the defeated there is no consolation in looking at the higher place on the podium, and congratulating the one who has beaten us. Even if we win, it is only for now, and we must start again from scratch next match, next year, next championship. Defeat is inevitable, for though we may beat the clock, we cannot beat time.

These texts are chosen for their linking of defeat and victory. Ring Lardner's story is that of the champion for whom victory is won with the complete absence of respect and honour. A. E. Housman's dead athlete will never see himself beaten. Atalanta, both young marriageable woman and unbeatable athlete, knows that fulfilment entails both success and failure; to win she must lose. Ovid shows us that each outcome is both itself and its opposite. Nick Hornby explores the curious phenomenon of how a deserved defeat can further cement an already absolute sense of identity; embattled football fans will recognise the deep sense of hurt following a defeat, and how unlikely it is that a defeat, or years of defeat, will lead anyone to support a different club.

But even success may not make us feel like winners – Byron's successful attempt to outdo Leander brought him not laurels but a fever.

RING LARDNER

From *Champion* (1916)

The brothers Haley were lunching in a Boston hotel. Dan had come down from Holyoke to visit with Tommy and to watch the latter's protegé go twelve rounds, or less, with Bud Cross. The bout promised little in the way of a contest, for Midge had twice stopped the Baltimore youth, and Bud's reputation for gameness was all that had earned him the date. The fans were willing to pay the price to see Midge's hay-making left, but they wanted to see it used on an opponent who would not jump out of the ring the first time he felt its crushing force. But Cross was such an opponent, and his willingness to stop boxing-gloves with his eyes, ears, nose and throat had long enabled him to escape the horrors of honest labour. A game boy was Bud, and he showed it in his battered, swollen, discoloured face.

'I should think,' said Dan Haley, 'that the kid'd do whatever you tell him after all you done for him.'

'Well,' said Tommy, 'he's took my dope pretty straight so far, but he's so sure of hisself that he can't see no reason for waitin'. He'll do what I say, though; he'd be a sucker not to.'

'You got a contrac' with him?'

'No, I don't need no contrac'. He knows it was me that drug him out o' the gutter and he ain't goin' to turn me down now, when he's got the dough and bound to get more. Where'd he of been at if I hadn't listened to him when he first come to me? That's pretty near two years ago now, but it seems like last week. I was settin' in the s'loon across from the Pleasant Club in Philly, waitin' for McCann to count the dough and come over, when this little bum blowed in and tried to stand the house off for a drink. They told him nothin' doin' and to beat it out o' there, and then he seen me and come over to where I was settin' and ast me wasn't I a boxin' man and I told him who I was. Then he ast me for money to buy a shot and I told him to set down and I'd buy it for him. Then we got talkin' things over and he told me his name and told me about fightn' a couple o' prelims out to Milwaukee. So I says, 'Well, boy, I don't know how good or how rotten you are, but you won't never get nowheres trainin' on that stuff.' So he says he'd cut it out if he could get on in a bout and I says I would give him a chance if he played square with me and didn't touch no more to drink. So we shook hands and I took him up to the hotel with me and give him a bath and the next day I bought him some clo'es. And I staked him to eats and sleeps for over six weeks. He had a hard time breakin' away from the polish, but finally I thought he was fit and I give him his chance. He went on with Smiley Sayer and stopped him so quick that Smiley thought sure he was poisoned.

'Well, you know what he's did since. The only beatin' in his record was by Tracy in Milwaukee before I got hold of him, and he's licked Tracy three times in the last year.

'I've gave him all the best of it in a money way and he's got seven thousand bucks in cold storage. How's that for a kid that was in the gutter two years ago? And he'd have still more yet if he wasn't so nuts over clo'es and got to stop at the good hotels and so forth.'

'Where's his home at?'

'Well, he ain't really got no home. He came from Chicago and his mother canned him out o' the house for bein' no good. She give him a raw deal, I guess, and he says he won't have nothin' to do with her unlest she comes to him first. She's got a pile o' money, he says, so he ain't worryin' about her.'

The gentleman under discussion entered the cafe and swaggered to Tommy's table, while the whole room turned to look.

Midge was the picture of health despite a slightly coloured eye and an ear that seemed to have no opening. But perhaps it was not his healthiness that drew all eyes. His diamond horse-shoe tie pin,

his purple cross-striped shirt, his orange shoes and his light blue suit fairly screamed for attention.

'Where you been?' he asked Tommy. 'I been lookin' all over for you.'

'Set down,' said his manager.

'No time,' said Midge. 'I'm goin' down to the w'arf and see 'em unload the fish.'

'Shake hands with my brother Dan,' said Tommy. Midge shook with the Holyoke Haley.

'If you're Tommy's brother, you're O.K. with me,' said Midge, and the brothers beamed with pleasure.

Dan moistened his lips and murmured an embarrassed reply, but it was lost on the young gladiator.

'Leave me take twenty,' Midge was saying. 'I prob'ly won't need it, but I don't like to be caught short.'

Tommy parted with a twenty dollar bill and recorded the transaction in a small black book the insurance company had given him for Christmas.

'But,' he said, 'it won't cost you no twenty to look at them fish. Want me to go along?'

'No,' said Midge hastily. 'You and your brother here prob'ly got a lot to say to each other.'

'Well,' said Tommy, 'don't take no bad money and don't get lost. And you better be back at four o'clock and lay down a w'ile.' 'I don't need no rest to beat this guy,' said Midge. 'He'll do enough layin' down for the both of us.'

And laughing even more than the jest called for, he strode out through the fire of admiring and startled glances.

A. E. HOUSMAN

To an Athlete Dying Young (1896)

THE time you won your town the race
We chaired you through the market-place;
Man and boy stood cheering by,
And home we brought you shoulder-high.

Today, the road all runners come,
Shoulder-high we bring you home,
And set you at your threshold down,
Townsman of a stiller town.

Smart lad, to slip betimes away
From fields where glory does not stay,
And early though the laurel grows
It withers quicker than the rose.

Eyes the shady night has shut
Cannot see the record cut,
And silence sounds no worse than cheers
After earth has stopped the ears:

Now you will not swell the rout
Of lads that wore their honours out,
Runners whom renown outran
And the name died before the man.

So set, before its echoes fade,
The fleet foot on the sill of shade,
And hold to the low lintel up
The still-defended challenge-cup.

And round that early-laurelled head
Will flock to gaze the strengthless dead,
And find unwithered on its curls
The garland briefer than a girl's.

OVID

From *Metamorphoses*, translated by John Dryden (1913)

Perhaps thou may'st have heard a virgin's name,
Who still in swiftness swiftest youths o'ercame.
Wondrous! that female weakness should outdo
A manly strength; the wonder yet is true.
'Twas doubtful, if her triumphs in the field
Did to her form's triumphant glories yield;
Whether her face could with more ease decoy
A crowd of lovers, or her feet destroy.
For once Apollo she implor'd to show
If courteous Fates a consort would allow:
A consort brings thy ruin, he reply'd;
O! learn to want the pleasures of a bride!
Nor shalt thou want them to thy wretched cost,
And Atalanta living shall be lost.
With such a rueful Fate th' affrighted maid
Sought green recesses in the woodland glade.
Nor sighing suiters her resolves could move,
She bad them show their speed, to show their love.
He only, who could conquer in the race,
Might hope the conquer'd virgin to embrace;
While he, whose tardy feet had lagg'd behind,
Was doom'd the sad reward of death to find.
Tho' great the prize, yet rigid the decree,
But blind with beauty, who can rigour see?
Ev'n on these laws the fair they rashly sought,
And danger in excess of love forgot.

There sat Hippomenes, prepar'd to blame
In lovers such extravagance of flame.
And must, he said, the blessing of a wife
Be dearly purchas'd by a risk of life?
But when he saw the wonders of her face,
And her limbs naked, springing to the race,
Her limbs, as exquisitely turn'd, as mine,
Or if a woman thou, might vie with thine,
With lifted hands, he cry'd, forgive the tongue
Which durst, ye youths, your well-tim'd courage wrong.
I knew not that the nymph, for whom you strove,
Deserv'd th' unbounded transports of your love.
He saw, admir'd, and thus her spotless frame
He prais'd, and praising, kindled his own flame.
A rival now to all the youths who run,
Envious, he fears they should not be undone.
But why (reflects he) idly thus is shown
The fate of others, yet untry'd my own?
The coward must not on love's aid depend;
The God was ever to the bold a friend.
Mean-time the virgin flies, or seems to fly,
Swift as a Scythian arrow cleaves the sky:
Still more and more the youth her charms admires.
The race itself t' exalt her charms conspires.
The golden pinions, which her feet adorn,
In wanton flutt'rings by the winds are born.
Down from her head, the long, fair tresses flow,
And sport with lovely negligence below.
The waving ribbands, which her buskins tie,
Her snowy skin with waving purple die;
As crimson veils in palaces display'd,
To the white marble lend a blushing shade.
Nor long he gaz'd, yet while he gaz'd, she gain'd

The goal, and the victorious wreath obtain'd.
The vanquish'd sigh, and, as the law decreed,
Pay the dire forfeit, and prepare to bleed.

Then rose Hippomenes, not yet afraid,
And fix'd his eyes full on the beauteous maid.
Where is (he cry'd) the mighty conquest won,
To distance those, who want the nerves to run?
Here prove superior strength, nor shall it be
Thy loss of glory, if excell'd by me.
High my descent, near Neptune I aspire,
For Neptune was grand-parent to my sire.
From that great God the fourth my self I trace,
Nor sink my virtues yet beneath my race.
Thou from Hippomenes, o'ercome, may'st claim
An envy'd triumph, and a deathless fame.

While thus the youth the virgin pow'r defies,
Silent she views him still with softer eyes.
Thoughts in her breast a doubtful strife begin,
If 'tis not happier now to lose, than win.
What God, a foe to beauty, would destroy
The promis'd ripeness of this blooming boy?
With his life's danger does he seek my bed?
Scarce am I half so greatly worth, she said.
Nor has his beauty mov'd my breast to love,
And yet, I own, such beauty well might move:
'Tis not his charms, 'tis pity would engage
My soul to spare the greenness of his age.
What, that heroick conrage fires his breast,
And shines thro' brave disdain of Fate confest?
What, that his patronage by close degrees
Springs from th' imperial ruler of the seas?

Then add the love, which bids him undertake
The race, and dare to perish for my sake.
Of bloody nuptials, heedless youth, beware!
Fly, timely fly from a too barb'rous fair.
At pleasure chuse; thy love will be repaid
By a less foolish, and more beauteous maid.
But why this tenderness, before unknown?
Why beats, and pants my breast for him alone?
His eyes have seen his num'rous rivals yield;
Let him too share the rigour of the field,
Since, by their fates untaught, his own he courts,
And thus with ruin insolently sports.
Yet for what crime shall he his death receive?
Is it a crime with me to wish to live?
Shall his kind passion his destruction prove?
Is this the fatal recompence of love?
So fair a youth, destroy'd, would conquest shame,
Aud nymphs eternally detest my fame.
Still why should nymphs my guiltless fame upbraid?
Did I the fond adventurer persuade?
Alas! I wish thou would'st the course decline,
Or that my swiftness was excell'd by thine.
See! what a virgin's bloom adorns the boy!
Why wilt thou run, and why thy self destroy?
Hippomenes! O that I ne'er had been
By those bright eyes unfortunately seen!
Ah! tempt not thus a swift, untimely Fate;
Thy life is worthy of the longest date.
Were I less wretched, did the galling chain
Of rigid Gods not my free choice restrain,
By thee alone I could with joy be led
To taste the raptures of a nuptial bed.

Thus she disclos'd the woman's secret heart,
Young, innocent, and new to Cupid's dart.
Her thoughts, her words, her actions wildly rove,
With love she burns, yet knows not that 'tis love.

Her royal sire now with the murm'ring crowd
Demands the race impatiently aloud.
Hippomenes then with true fervour pray'd,
My bold attempt let Venus kindly aid.
By her sweet pow'r I felt this am'rous fire,
Still may she succour, whom she did inspire.

A soft, unenvious wind, with speedy care,
Wafted to Heav'n the lover's tender pray'r.
Pity, I own, soon gain'd the wish'd consent,
And all th' assistance he implor'd I lent.
The Cyprian lands, tho' rich, in richness yield
To that, surnam'd the Tamasenian field.
That field of old was added to my shrine,
And its choice products consecrated mine.
A tree there stands, full glorious to behold,
Gold are the leafs, the crackling branches gold.
It chanc'd, three apples in my hand I bore,
Which newly from the tree I sportive tore;
Seen by the youth alone, to him I brought
The fruit, and when, and how to use it, taught.
The signal sounding by the king's command,
Both start at once, and sweep th' imprinted sand.
So swiftly mov'd their feet, they might with ease,
Scarce moisten'd, skim along the glassy seas;
Or with a wondrous levity be born
O'er yellow harvests of unbending corn.
Now fav'ring peals resound from ev'ry part,
Spirit the youth, and fire his fainting heart.
Hippomenes! (they cry'd) thy life preserve,
Intensely labour, and stretch ev'ry nerve.
Base fear alone can baffle thy design,
Shoot boldly onward, and the goal is thine.
'Tis doubtful whether shouts, like these, convey'd
More pleasures to the youth, or to the maid.
When a long distance oft she could have gain'd,
She check'd her swiftness, and her feet restrain'd:
She sigh'd, and dwelt, and languish'd on his face,
Then with unwilling speed pursu'd the race.
O'er-spent with heat, his breath he faintly drew,

Parch'd was his mouth, nor yet the goal in view,
And the first apple on the plain he threw.
The nymph stop'd sudden at th' unusual sight,
Struck with the fruit so beautifully bright.
Aside she starts, the wonder to behold,
And eager stoops to catch the rouling gold.
Th' observant youth past by, and scour'd along,
While peals of joy rung from th' applauding throng.
Unkindly she corrects the short delay,
And to redeem the time fleets swift away,
Swift, as the lightning, or the northern wind,
And far she leaves the panting youth behind.
Again he strives the flying nymph to hold
With the temptation of the second gold:
The bright temptation fruitlessly was tost,
So soon, alas! she won the distance lost.
Now but a little interval of space
Remain'd for the decision of the race.
Fair author of the precious gift, he said,
Be thou, O Goddess, author of my aid!
Then of the shining fruit the last he drew,
And with his full-collected vigour threw:
The virgin still the longer to detain,
Threw not directly, but a-cross the plain.
She seem'd a-while perplex'd in dubious thought,
If the far-distant apple should be sought:
I lur'd her backward mind to seize the bait,
And to the massie gold gave double weight.
My favour to my votary was show'd,
Her speed I lessen'd, and encreas'd her load.
But lest, tho' long, the rapid race be run,
Before my longer, tedious tale is done,
The youth the goal, and so the virgin won.

NICK HORNBY

From *Fever Pitch* (1992)

West Ham v Arsenal
10.5.80

Everyone knows the song that Millwall fans sing, to the tune of 'Sailing': 'No one likes us/No one likes us/No one likes us/ We don't care.' In fact I have always felt that the song is a little melodramatic, and that if anyone should sing it, it is Arsenal.

Every Arsenal fan, the youngest and the oldest, is aware that no one likes us, and every day we hear that dislike reiterated. The average media-attuned football fan – someone who reads a sports page most days, watches TV whenever it is on, reads a fanzine or a football magazine – will come across a slighting reference to Arsenal maybe two or three times a week (about as often as he or she will hear a Lennon and McCartney song, I would guess). I have just finished watching *Saint and Greavsie*, during the course of which Jimmy Greaves thanked the Wrexham manager for 'delighting millions' with the Fourth Division team's victory over us in the FA Cup; the cover of a football magazine kicking around in the flat promises an article entitled 'Why does everyone hate Arsenal?' Last week there was an article in a national newspaper attacking our players for their lack of artistry; one of the players thus abused was eighteen years old and hadn't even played for the first team at the time.

We're boring, and lucky, and dirty, and petulant, and rich, and mean, and have been, as far as I can tell, since the 1930s. That was when the greatest football manager of all time, Herbert Chapman, introduced an extra defender and changed the way football was played, thus founding Arsenal's reputation for negative, unattractive football; yet successive Arsenal teams, notably the Double team in 1971, used an intimidatingly competent defence as a springboard for success. (Thirteen of our league games that year ended nil–nil or 1–0, and it is fair to say that none of them were pretty.) I would guess that 'Lucky Arsenal' was born out of 'Boring Arsenal', in that sixty years of 1–0 wins tend to test the credulity and patience of opposing fans.

West Ham, on the other hand, like Tottenham, are famous for their poetry and flair and commitment to good, fluent ('progressive', in the current argot, a word which for those of us in our thirties is distressingly reminiscent of Emerson, Lake and Palmer and King Crimson) football. Everyone has a soft spot for Peters and Moore and Hurst and Brooking and the West Ham 'Academy', just as everyone loathes and despises Storey and Talbot and Adams and the whole idea and purpose of Arsenal. No matter that the wild-eyed Martin Allen and the brutish Julian Dicks currently represent the Hammers, just as Van Den Hauwe and Fenwick and Edinburgh represent Spurs. No matter that the gifted Merson and the dazzling Limpar play for Arsenal. No matter that in 1989 and 1992 we scored more goals than anyone else in the First Division. The Hammers and the Lilleywhites are the Keepers of the Flame, the Only Followers of the True Path; we are the Gunners, the Visigoths, with King Herod and the Sheriff of Nottingham as our twin centre-halves, their arms in the air appealing for offside.

West Ham, Arsenal's opponents in the 1980 Cup Final, were in the Second Division that season, and their lowly status made people drool over them even more. To the nation's delight, Arsenal lost. Saint Trevor of England scored the only goal and slew the odious monster, the Huns were repelled, children could sleep safely in their beds again. So what are we left with, us Arsenal fans, who for most of our lives have allowed ourselves to become identified with the villains? Nothing; and our sense of stoicism and grievance is almost thrilling.

The only things anyone remembers about the game now are

Brooking's rare headed goal, and Willie Young's monstrous professional foul on Paul Allen, just as the youngest player to appear in a Cup Final was about to score one of the cutest and most romantic goals ever seen at Wembley. Standing on the Wembley terraces among the silent, embarrassed Arsenal fans, deafened by the boos that came from the West Ham end and the neutrals in the stadium, I was appalled by Young's cynicism.

But that night, watching the highlights on TV, I became aware that a part of me actually enjoyed the foul – not because it stopped Allen from scoring (the game was over, we'd lost, and that hardly mattered), but because it was so comically, parodically *Arsenalesque*. Who else but an Arsenal defender would have clattered a tiny seventeen-year-old member of the Academy? Motson or Davies, I can't remember which, was suitably disgusted and pompous about it all; to me, sick of hearing about how the goodies had put the baddies to flight, his righteousness sounded provocative. There was something about it that reminded me of Bill Grundy winding up the Sex Pistols on television in 1976 and then expressing his outrage about their behaviour afterwards. Arsenal, the first of the true punk rockers: our centre-halves were fulfilling a public need for harmless pantomime deviancy long before Johnny Rotten came along.

LORD BYRON

Written after Swimming from Sestos to Abydos **(1881)**

If, in the month of dark December,
Leander, who was nightly wont
(What maid will not the tale remember?)
To cross thy stream, broad Hellespont!

If, when the wintry tempest roared,
He sped to Hero, nothing loath,
And thus of old thy current poured,
Fair Venus! how I pity both!

For me, degenerate modern wretch,
Though in the genial month of May,
My dripping limbs I faintly stretch,
And think I've done a feat today.

But since he crossed the rapid tide,
According to the doubtful story,
To woo – and – Lord knows what beside,
And swam for Love, as I for Glory;

'Twere hard to say who fared the best:
Sad mortals! thus the gods still plague you!
He lost his labour, I my jest;
For he was drowned, and I've the ague.

4

WINNING

We will always have that moment, that minute when we were gods. Fairly won, the medal in its box, the name on the cup, they are all moments in history that can never be changed. And there has to be a place in a sporting anthology for winners, champions and heroes, the ones who broke the tape and the record.

Norman Gale's The Church Cricketant and the passages from Ivanhoe and Tom Brown's Schooldays are unashamed stories of the delight of winning and the roar of the crowd. The same, in a do-it-yourself sort of way, is offered by Garrison Keillor. Even without knowing baseball terminology it is easy to recognise the question he poses here: exactly how serious should we be about sport?

Walter Thom describes Captain Robert Barclay's walking race, in a challenge against an old adversary who had beaten him twice. The challenge on this occasion in 1801 was that Captain Barclay would walk 90 miles within 21 hours, for a prize of five thousand guineas (around two million pounds in today's money). Barclay's most celebrated feat was a walk of a thousand miles in a thousand successive hours between 1 June and 12 July 1809. Such athletic challenges were a major part of sporting life in the early nineteenth century, and far more important than cricket or football. The excitement of nineteenth-century boxing is also captured here in colourful terms by Pierce Egan. Boxers and pedestrians were folk heroes, and the successful ones became wealthy celebrities. It is difficult not to feel exhilarated by Egan's breathless prose.

Captain Barclay's records were based on hard work, will and preparation. Willpower and opportunism lie behind Arthur Machin's success in David Storey's portrayal of the relationship between ambition and winning. Being a winner means competing successfully, whatever it takes. Winning, as we know, is everything.

SIR WALTER SCOTT

From *Ivanhoe* (1820)

The sound of the trumpets soon recalled those spectators who had already begun to leave the field; and proclamation was made that Prince John, suddenly called by high and peremptory public duties, held himself obliged to discontinue the entertainments of tomorrow's festival: Nevertheless, that, unwilling so many good yeoman should depart without a trial of skill, he was pleased to appoint them, before leaving the ground, presently to execute the competition of archery intended for the morrow. To the best archer a prize was to be awarded, being a bugle-horn, mounted with silver, and a silken baldric richly ornamented with a medallion of St Hubert, the patron of silvan sport.

More than thirty yeomen at first presented themselves as competitors, several of whom were rangers and under-keepers in the royal forests of Needwood and Charnwood. When, however, the archers understood with whom they were to be matched, upwards of twenty withdrew themselves from the contest, unwilling to encounter the dishonour of almost certain defeat. For in those days the skill of each celebrated marksman was as well known for many miles round him, as the qualities of a horse trained at Newmarket are familiar to those who frequent that well-known meeting.

The diminished list of competitors for silvan fame still amounted to eight. Prince John stepped from his royal seat to view more nearly the persons of these chosen yeomen, several of whom wore the royal livery. Having satisfied his curiosity by this investigation, he looked for the object of his resentment, whom he observed standing on the same spot, and with the same composed countenance which he had exhibited upon the preceding day.

'Fellow,' said Prince John, 'I guessed by thy insolent babble that thou wert no true lover of the longbow, and I see thou darest not adventure thy skill among such merry-men as stand yonder.'

'Under favour, sir,' replied the yeoman, 'I have another reason for refraining to shoot, besides the fearing discomfiture and disgrace.'

'And what is thy other reason?' said Prince John, who, for some cause which perhaps he could not himself have explained, felt a painful curiosity respecting this individual.

'Because,' replied the woodsman, 'I know not if these yeomen and I are used to shoot at the same marks; and because, moreover, I know not how your Grace might relish the winning of a third prize by one who has unwittingly fallen under your displeasure.'

Prince John coloured as he put the question, 'What is thy name, yeoman?'

'Locksley,' answered the yeoman.

'Then, Locksley,' said Prince John, 'thou shalt shoot in thy turn, when these yeomen have displayed their skill. If thou carriest the prize, I will add to it twenty nobles; but if thou losest it, thou shalt be stript of thy Lincoln green, and scourged out of the lists with bowstrings, for a wordy and insolent braggart.'

'And how if I refuse to shoot on such a wager?' said the yeoman. 'Your Grace's power, supported, as it is, by so many men-at-arms, may indeed easily strip and scourge me, but cannot compel me to bend or to draw my bow.'

'If thou refusest my fair proffer,' said the Prince, 'the Provost of the lists shall cut thy bowstring, break thy bow and arrows, and expel thee from the presence as a faint-hearted craven.'

'This is no fair chance you put on me, proud Prince,' said the yeoman, 'to compel me to peril myself against the best archers of Leicester and Staffordshire, under the penalty of infamy if they should overshoot me. Nevertheless, I will obey your pleasure.'

'Look to him close, men-at-arms,' said Prince John, 'his heart is sinking; I am jealous lest he attempt to escape the trial. – And do you, good fellows, shoot boldly round; a buck and a butt of wine are ready for your refreshment in yonder tent, when the prize is won.'

A target was placed at the upper end of the southern avenue which led to the lists. The contending archers took their station in turn, at the bottom of the southern access, the distance between that station and the mark allowing full distance for what was called a shot at rovers. The archers, having previously determined by lot their order of precedence, were to shoot each three shafts in succession. The sports were regulated by an officer of inferior rank, termed the Provost of the Games; for the high rank of the marshals of the lists would have been held degraded, had they condescended to superintend the sports of the yeomanry.

One by one the archers, stepping forward, delivered their shafts yeomanlike and bravely. Of twenty-four arrows, shot in succession, ten were fixed in the target, and the others ranged so near it, that, considering the distance of the mark, it was accounted good archery. Of the ten shafts which hit the target, two within the inner ring were shot by Hubert, a forester in the service of Malvoisin, who was accordingly pronounced victorious.

'Now, Locksley,' said Prince John to the bold yeoman, with a bitter smile, 'wilt thou try conclusions with Hubert, or wilt thou yield up bow, baldric, and quiver, to the Provost of the sports?'

'Sith it be no better,' said Locksley, 'I am content to try my fortune; on condition that when I have shot two shafts at yonder mark of Hubert's, he shall be bound to shoot one at that which I shall propose.'

'That is but fair,' answered Prince John, 'and it shall not be refused thee. – If thou dost beat this braggart, Hubert, I will fill the bugle with silver-pennies for thee.'

'A man can do but his best,' answered Hubert; 'but my grandsire drew a good long bow at Hastings, and I trust not to dishonour his memory.'

The former target was now removed, and a fresh one of the

same size placed in its room. Hubert, who, as victor in the first trial of skill, had the right to shoot first, took his aim with great deliberation, long measuring the distance with his eye, while he held in his hand his bended bow, with the arrow placed on the string. At length he made a step forward, and raising the bow at the full stretch of his left arm, till the centre or grasping-place was nigh level with his face, he drew his bowstring to his ear. The arrow whistled through the air, and lighted within the inner ring of the target, but not exactly in the centre.

'You have not allowed for the wind, Hubert,' said his antagonist, bending his bow, 'or that had been a better shot.'

So saying, and without showing the least anxiety to pause upon his aim, Locksley stept to the appointed station, and shot his arrow as carelessly in appearance as if he had not even looked at the mark. He was speaking almost at the instant that the shaft left the bowstring, yet it alighted in the target two inches nearer to the white spot which marked the centre than that of Hubert.

'By the light of heaven!' said Prince John to Hubert, 'an thou suffer that runagate knave to overcome thee, thou art worthy of the gallows!'

Hubert had but one set speech for all occasions. 'An your highness were to hang me,' he said, 'a man can but do his best. Nevertheless, my grandsire drew a good bow –'

'The foul fiend on thy grandsire and all his generation!' interrupted John, 'shoot, knave, and shoot thy best, or it shall be the worse for thee!'

Thus exhorted, Hubert resumed his place, and not neglecting the caution which he had received from his adversary, he made the necessary allowance for a very light air of wind, which had just arisen, and shot so successfully that his arrow alighted in the very centre of the target.

'A Hubert! a Hubert!' shouted the populace, more interested in a known person than in a stranger. 'In the clout! – in the clout! – a

Hubert for ever!'

'Thou canst not mend that shot, Locksley,' said the Prince, with an insulting smile.

'I will notch his shaft for him, however,' replied Locksley.

And letting fly his arrow with a little more precaution than before, it lighted right upon that of his competitor, which it split to shivers. The people who stood around were so astonished at his wonderful dexterity, that they could not even give vent to their surprise in their usual clamour. 'This must be the devil, and no man of flesh and blood,' whispered the yeomen to each other; 'such archery was never seen since a bow was first bent in Britain.'

'And now,' said Locksley, 'I will crave your Grace's permission to plant such a mark as is used in the North Country; and welcome every brave yeoman who shall try a shot at it to win a smile from the bonny lass he loves best.'

He then turned to leave the lists. 'Let your guards attend me,' he said, 'if you please – I go but to cut a rod from the next willow-bush.'

Prince John made a signal that some attendants should follow him in case of his escape: but the cry of 'Shame! shame!' which burst from the multitude, induced him to alter his ungenerous purpose.

Locksley returned almost instantly with a willow wand about six feet in length, perfectly straight, and rather thicker than a man's thumb. He began to peel this with great composure, observing at the same time that to ask a good woodsman to shoot at a target so broad as had hitherto been used was to put shame upon his skill. 'For his own part,' he said, 'and in the land where he was bred, men would as soon take for their mark King Arthur's round-table, which held sixty knights around it. A child of seven years old,' he said, 'might hit yonder target with a headless shaft; but,' added he, walking deliberately to the other end of the lists, and sticking the willow wand upright in the ground, 'he that hits that rod at five-score yards, I call him an archer fit to bear both bow and quiver before a king, an it were the stout King Richard himself.'

'My grandsire,' said Hubert, 'drew a good bow at the battle of Hastings, and never shot at such a mark in his life – and neither will I. If this yeoman can cleave that rod, I give him the bucklers – or rather, I yield to the devil that is in his jerkin, and not to any human skill; a man can but do his best, and I will not shoot where I am sure to miss. I might as well shoot at the edge of our parson's whittle, or at a wheat straw, or at a sunbeam, as at a twinkling white streak which I can hardly see.'

'Cowardly dog!' said Prince John. 'Sirrah Locksley, do thou shoot; but, if thou hittest such a mark, I will say thou art the first man ever did so. However it be, thou shalt not crow over us with a mere show of superior skill.'

'I will do my best, as Hubert says,' answered Locksley; 'no man can do more.'

So saying, he again bent his bow, but on the present occasion looked with attention to his weapon, and changed the string, which he thought was no longer truly round, having been a little frayed by the two former shots. He then took his aim with some deliberation, and the multitude awaited the event in breathless silence. The archer vindicated their opinion of his skill: his arrow split the willow rod against which it was aimed. A jubilee of acclamations followed; and even Prince John, in admiration of Locksley's skill, lost for an instant his dislike to his person. 'These twenty nobles,' he said, 'which, with the bugle, thou hast fairly won, are thine own; we will make them fifty, if thou wilt take livery and service with us as a yeoman of our body guard, and be near to our person. For never did so strong a hand bend a bow, or so true an eye direct a shaft.'

'Pardon me, noble Prince,' said Locksley; 'but I have vowed, that if ever I take service, it should be with your royal brother King Richard. These twenty nobles I leave to Hubert, who has this day drawn as brave a bow as his grandsire did at Hastings. Had his modesty not refused the trial, he would have hit the wand as well as I.'

Hubert shook his head as he received with reluctance the bounty of the stranger, and Locksley, anxious to escape further observation, mixed with the crowd, and was seen no more.

The victorious archer would not perhaps have escaped John's attention so easily, had not that Prince had other subjects of anxious and more important meditation pressing upon his mind at that instant. He called upon his chamberlain as he gave the signal for retiring from the lists, and commanded him instantly to gallop to Ashby, and seek out Isaac the Jew. 'Tell the dog,' he said, 'to send me, before sun-down, two thousand crowns. He knows the security; but thou mayst show him this ring for a token. The rest of the money must be paid at York within six days. If he neglects, I will have the unbelieving villain's head. Look that thou pass him not on the way; for the circumcised slave was displaying his stolen finery amongst us.'

So saying, the Prince resumed his horse, and returned to Ashby, the whole crowd breaking up and dispersing upon his retreat.

PIERCE EGAN

From *Boxiana, or Sketches of Ancient and Modern Pugilism* (1824)

HICKMAN is a well-made, compact man, and does not appear, on viewing him, near so heavy as he proves at the scales, weighing about 11 stone 11 pounds. He is in height about 5 feet 9½ inches. His *nob* is a fighting one and his eyes are small, but protected by prominent forehead. His frame, when stripped, is firm and round, and displays considerable muscular strength. HICKMAN is very active upon his legs. He is not a *showy*, but an effective, decisive hitter; perhaps, the term of *smashing* boxer would be more appropriate, and near his real character. He is, however, a much better fighter than he looks to be; his blows are tremendous, and of most *punishing* quality towards victory. HICKMAN possesses all the *confidence* of Nelson, united with the *desperation* of a *Paul Jones*. In short, he appears to be one of those sort of beings well calculated to mix with the ruder elements of society – one who can listen to the howlings of the furious tempest, and also stand unmoved from the effects of the pitiless pelting storm.

We believe it was owing to *Tom Shelton* (who first discovered this *milling diamond* in the rough) that he exhibited in the Prize Ring. *The out-and-out* qualities of HICKMAN, it should seem, were *whispered* to a few of the judges *on the sly*, and a patron was at length found for him. It was then determined that he should be *tried* with a promising young hero; and the following match was made between HICKMAN and *Crawley*, for £50 a-side, which took place on Tuesday, March 16, 1819, at Moulsey Hurst.

THE FANCY, so far from being *chilled* by their last *dripping wet* excursion to the Barge House, it appears, *panted* high for the arrival of another day's sport. The morning was rather *loury*, but the

enlivening rays of bright *Sol* at length chased away all gloom, and infused, animation, interest, and *spirits*, throughout the whole of the amateurs. It might be termed the first *turn-out* of the FANCY for the spring season and the vehicles were gay and elegant. The presence of some of the *Corinthians* gave importance to the scene; *Swells* of the second-rate order of the amateurs were also numerous and scarcely any *drags* or *tumblers* were to be witnessed loaded with '*the lads!*' In fact, it was a superior cut altogether. More interest was excited upon the fight than might have been expected, when both the boxers, in point of *trial*, were viewed as new ones to the ring. HICKMAN, although a *light subject* in himself, was, to the amateurs, completely a *dark one*, respecting his merits or his person. '*What sort of CHAP is he? What has he done? Has he ever fought anybody?*' were repeatedly asked and as repeatedly answered, '*that no one knew any thing about him.*' It was, however, generally understood that he was very *strong*; but it was urged, as a sort of drawback, that he had too much *chaffing* about his composition. On the contrary, young *Rump Steak* stood high as a *muffler*; and it was known he had beat one of the *cutting-up* tribe, but who turned out a mere *cripple* as a fighting man. His strength and stamina were doubted; he was a youth of not more than 19 years of age, nearly six feet high, 12 stone in weight, but thought to have more *gristle* than bone: his *victualling office* had also been some time out of *commission*; however, the keen air of Hampstead, added to good *grubbery*, had not only produced an improvement of his *frame*, but had reduced the odds against him, and, on the morning of fighting, it was, in a great measure, *even betting*. The importance of the man of gas was kept up by his *trainer, Shelton*, who confidently asserted that if HICKMAN did not win, he would quit the boxing ring and take up a *quiet abode* with OLD NEPTUNE; *Oliver* coinciding in the same opinion. Such was the state of affairs till the moment arrived for the appearance of the heroes on the *plains of Moulsey*. HICKMAN showed first in the ring, and threw up his *castor* jolly, very *jolly* indeed, attended by his seconds, *Oliver* and *Shelton*; and *Crawley* soon followed, repeating the token of defiance, waited upon by *Painter* and *Jones*. The colours were tied to the stakes and, at one o'clock, the men *set to*.

First round. – The *gas-light* blade seemed a well *primed* four-pound burner, and eager to eclipse his opponent with his superior rays of brilliancy. He showed fight instantly, rushed upon his opponent, and gave young Rump-steak *mugger*, but it did not prove effective. Crawley endeavoured to retreat from the *boring* qualities of his antagonist, and *tapped* HICKMAN over his guard. The latter went in almost laughing at the *science* against him and Crawley could not resist his efforts with any tiling like a *stopper*. He also received a desperate hit upon his right ear, that not only drew forth the *claret*, but *floored* him. In going down, he unfortunately hit his head against the stakes. '*Well done, my gassy*' from the light company; and 7 to 4 was offered upon him.

Second. – The appearance of Crawley was completely altered. He was quite *groggy* from the united effects of the last blow and the stakes. The Gas Man let fly *sans ceremonie*, and the *nob* of his opponent was *pinked* in all directions. His nose sustained a heavy hit, and he went down covered with *claret*. Ten pounds to five upon HICKMAN.

Third. – It was evident that Crawley had not strength enough in the first round, but now he was quite reduced. He, however, showed good pluck, put in some hits that marked his opponent, and swelled up his left eye like a roll; but he was punished in return dreadfully, and again went down. 15 to 5, but no takers.

Fourth. – Crawley received a terrible hit in the throat, fell down on his back, with his arms extended, and quite exhausted. 5 to 1.

Fifth. – Crawley set to with more spirit than could possibly be expected. He planted some *facers* but the force of his opponent operated upon him like a torrent, and the stream appeared to carry him away. He was punished up to the ropes, and then *floored* upon his face. 7 to 1.

Sixth. – The *pluck* of Crawley was good, he tried to make change, but without effect, and received a *nobber* that sent him staggering away, quite abroad, when he fell down.

Seventh. – This was a desperate *game* round, and Crawley gave hit for hit till the Gas-Light Man's face blazed again. But Crawley was exhausted, and both went down. '*Go along, Crawley; such another round, and you can't lose it.*' It was a complete milling.

Eighth. – Crawley also fought manfully this round; but he had no chance, and the Gas Man again sent him down. All betters, but no takers.

Ninth. – The right hand of HICKMAN was tremendous. Crawley's *nob* completely in *Chancery*, and he was terribly *milled* out of the ring, bleeding in all directions.

Tenth. – This round was similar to the famous one between Painter and Sutton, during their first fight. Crawley was so severely hit from the scratch, that he never put up his hands. It was piteous to see him. '*Take him away!*' from all parts of the ring.

Eleventh. – This round was nearly as bad, but the *game* of young *Rump-steak* was much praised. The Gas Man did not go without some sharp punishment.

Twelfth. – Crawley floored in a twinkling and long, very long, before this period, it was '*Tom Cribb's Memorial to Congress*' to a *penny chaunt*; Crawley could not resist the heavy hitting of his opponent.

Thirteenth and last. – The Gas-Light Man had completely put his opponent in *darkness*; and he only appeared this round to be *smashed* all to pieces; or, as the French observe, to have the *coup de grace*. Thirteen minutes and a half *finished* poor Crawley!

THE GAS MAN retained all his *blaze*; in fact, he *burnt* brighter in his own opinion than before. However, he was pronounced, by the amateurs present, not a good fighter. Indeed, a few words will suffice. HICKMAN appeared fond of *rushing* forwards to *mill* his opponent, regardless of the result to himself. He hit with his left hand open. But no man could be on *better terms with himself* than HICKMAN was during the above fight. The good judges thought well of the GAS-LIGHT MAN, from the specimen he had displayed, yet urged he had great room for improvement but, when possessing the advantages of *science*, he would doubtless prove a *teazer* to all of his own, and even above his weight, *Crawley* had out-grown his strength.

In the above battle, in the third round, HICKMAN injured one of his hands materially indeed, so much did it operate on his feelings, from the severity of the pain, that he kept looking at one of his fingers, and complained of it to his second, *Tom Shelton*. The latter, with much *bluntness*, told him, 'to hold his *chaffing*; such conduct was not the way to win; and also that he was not hurt!' The GAS-LIGHT MAN took the hint, and was *silent* during the remainder of the battle. He also fought and won like hero. In a few days after the fight, his hand was so painful, and likewise had assumed such black appearance, that he was compelled to have the advice of a surgeon. The latter person, on examining his hand, found one of his fingers was broken. Upon this circumstance being made known to the amateurs, no doubt was entertained of his *game* qualities.

The GAS-LIGHT MAN was, from this conquest, looked upon as SOMEBODY by the *Fancy* and several matches were *talked* over for him; but they all *went off*, except the following contest, which was made up in very hasty manner, for purse of £20, at the Tennis-Court, at *Cy. Davis's* benefit.

HICKMAN, in consequence of the above meeting, entered the lists with the scientific *Cooper*, at Farnham Royal, Dawney Common, contiguous to Stowe House, near Stowe, Buckinghamshire, 24 miles from London, on Tuesday, March 28, 1820, immediately after *Cabbage* and *Martin* had left the ring. This contest was previously termed *fine science* against downright RUFFIANISM; and 7 to 4 and 2 to 1 was the current betting on *Cooper*, without the slightest hesitation. On entering the ring, the latter looked *pale*; but when he stripped, his frame had an elegant appearance; and he had for his seconds *Oliver* and *Bill Gibbons*. HICKMAN was under the guidance of *Randall* and *Shelton* and he laughed in the most confident manner, observing, 'that he was sure to win.' Previously to the combatants commencing the battle, Mr JACKSON called them both to him, stating the amount of the subscriptions he had collected for the winner. '*I am quite satisfied*' replied HICKMAN; '*I will fight, if it is only for a glass of gin!*' This sort of independence quite puzzled all the *Swells* and the GAS-LIGHT MAN was put down as great boaster, or an *out-and-outer* extraordinary: but, notwithstanding all this confidence manifested by HICKMAN, the well-known superior science possessed by *George Cooper* rendered him decidedly the favourite.

First round. – On setting-to, Cooper placed himself in an elegant position, and a few seconds passed away in sparring, and in his getting room to make play. Every eye was on the stretch, watching for the superiority of Cooper, but the rapidity of attack made by the Gas Man was so overwhelming, that he drove Cooper to the ropes, and the exchange of hits was terrific, till Cooper went down like a shot out of the ropes, from a terrible blow on the tip of his nose and his face was pinked all over. The shouting was tremendous: '*Bravo, Gas; it's all up with his science.*'

Second. – The *impetuosity* of the Gas-Light Man positively electrified the spectators and he went in to *mill* Cooper with all the indifference of being opposed to a complete *novice*. Cooper's face was quite changed. He seemed almost choked with the blood in his throat, and he was compelled to spit some of it out; but, nevertheless, as the Gas was coming in with downright ferocity, Cooper planted a tremendous *facer*, right in the middle of his head. This blow, heavy as it was, only made the Gas Man shake his head a little, as if he wished to throw something off it but, in renewing the attack, HICKMAN slipped down from a slight hit. Great shouting, and 'The Gas-Light Man is a rum one!' The odds had dropped materially, and HICKMAN was taken for choice.

Third. – The face of HICKMAN now showed the talents of

Cooper, and he was hit down on one knee but the former instantly jumped up to renew the attack, when Cooper set himself down on his second's knee, in order to finish the round.

Fourth. – Gas followed Cooper all over the ring, and hit him down. (Tumultuous shouting.) 2 to 1 on Gas.

Fifth. – The fine science of Cooper had its advantages in this round. He planted some desperate *facers* with great success and the *nob* of his opponent now bled profusely. In struggling for the throw, both down, but Gas undermost. By way of a cordial to Cooper, some of his friends shouted, 'Cooper for £100.'

Sixth. – This was a truly terrific round; and Cooper showed that he could hit tremendously, as well as his opponent. *Facer* for *facer* was exchanged without any fear or delay; and Cooper got away from some heavy blows. In closing, both down.

Seventh. – The qualities of the Gas-Light Man were so terrible, that Cooper with all his fine fighting, could not reduce his courage. HICKMAN would not be denied. The latter got *nobbed* prodigiously, and his *face* was covered with *claret*. In struggling for the throw, Cooper got his adversary down. '*Well done, George.*'

Eighth. – The Gas-Light Man now seemed to commence this round rather cautiously, and began to spar, as if for wind. '*If you spar,*' says Randall, '*you'll be licked. You must go and fight!*' The hitting on both sides was dreadful and the Gas Man got Cooper on the ropes, and *punished* him so terribly, that 'Foul!' and 'Fair!' was loudly vociferated, till Cooper went down quite weak.

Ninth. – The Gas-Light Man, from his impetuous mode of attack, appeared as if determined to *finish* Cooper off hand. The latter had scarcely left his second's knee, when HICKMAN ran up to him, and planted a severe *facer*. The appearance of Cooper was now piteous. He was quite feeble, nay, dead beat, till he was hit down.

Tenth. – In this round Cooper was hit down, quite exhausted, and picked up nearly senseless. 'It's all up,' was the cry and, in fact, so much was it felt round the ring, that numbers left their places, thinking it impossible for Cooper again to meet his antagonist. Any odds, but no takers.

Eleventh. – In the anxiety of the moment, several of the spectators thought the *time* rather long before it was called; and, to their great astonishment, Cooper, somehow or other, was again brought to the scratch. He was in a shockingly feeble state, but he nevertheless showed fight, till he was sent down. '*Bravo, Cooper*; you are a *game* fellow indeed!'

Twelfth. – This was most complete *ruffianing* round on both sides. The Gas-Light Man's *nob* was a picture of *punishment*. Cooper astonished the ring from the *gameness* he displayed, and the manly way in which he stood up to his adversary, giving hit for hit, till both went down.

Thirteenth. – It was evident that Cooper had never recovered from the severity of the blow he had received on the tip of his nose in the first round, and that, at times, he was almost choked with the blood in his throat. '*It's all up,*' was the cry, but Cooper fought in the most courageous style till he went down.

Fourteenth. – Cooper, although weak, was still a troublesome customer. He fought with his adversary, giving hit for hit, till he was quite exhausted and down.

Fifteenth. – This round was so well contested, as to claim admiration and praise from all parts of the ring, and '*Well done on both sides*' was loudly vociferated. Cooper was at length distressed beyond measure; but he nevertheless opposed HICKMAN with blow for blow, till Cooper went down.

Sixteenth, and last. – Without something like a miracle taking place, it was impossible for Cooper to win. He, however, manfully contended for victory, making exchanges, till both of the combatants went down. When 'Time' was called, HICKMAN appeared at the scratch, but Cooper was too exhausted to leave his second's knee; and HICKMAN was proclaimed the conqueror, amidst the shouts of his friends. The battle was over in the short space of FOURTEEN MINUTES AND A HALF!

GARRISON KEILLOR

Attitude (1979)

Long ago I passed the point in life when major-league ballplayers begin to be younger than yourself. Now all of them are, except for a few aging tri-genarians and a couple of quadros who don't get around on the fastball as well as they used to and who sit out the second games of double headers. However, despite my age (thirty-nine), I am still active and have a lot of interests. One of them is slow-pitch softball, a game that lets me go through the motions of baseball without getting beaned or having to run too hard. I play on a pretty casual team, one that drinks beer on the bench and substitutes freely. If a player's wife or girlfriend wants to play, we give her a glove and send her out to right field, no questions asked, and if she lets a pop fly drop six feet in front of her, nobody agonizes over it.

Except me. This year. For the first time in my life, just as I am entering the dark twilight of my slow-pitch career, I find myself taking the game seriously. It isn't the bonehead play that bothers me especially – the pop fly that drops untouched, the slow roller juggled and the ball then heaved ten feet over the first baseman's head and into the next diamond, the routine singles that go through outfielders' legs for doubles and triples with gloves flung after them. No, it isn't our stone-glove fielding or pussyfoot base-running or limp-wristed hitting that gives me fits, though these have put us on the short end of some mighty ridiculous scores this summer. It's our attitude.

Bottom of the ninth, down 18-3, two outs, a man on first and a woman on third, and our third baseman strikes out. Strikes out! In slow-pitch, not even your grandmother strikes out, but this guy does, and after his third strike – a wild swing at a ball that bounces on the plate – he topples over in the dirt and lies flat on his back, laughing. *Laughing!*

Same game, earlier. They have the bases loaded. A weak grounder is hit toward our second baseperson. The runners are running. She picks up the ball, and she looks at them. She looks at first, at second, at home. We yell, 'Throw it! Throw it!,' and she throws it, underhand, at the pitcher, who has turned and run to back up the catcher. The ball rolls across the third-base line and under the bench. Three runs score. The batter, a fatso, chugs into second. The other team hoots and hollers, and what does she do? She shrugs and smiles ('Oh, silly me'); after all, it's only a game. Like the aforementioned strikeout artist, she treats her error as a joke. They have forgiven themselves instantly, which is unforgivable. It is we who should forgive them, who can say, 'It's all right, it's only a game.' They are supposed to throw up their hands and kick the dirt and hang their heads, as if this boner, even if it is their sixteenth of the afternoon – this is the one that really and truly breaks their hearts.

That attitude sweetens the game for everyone. The sinner feels sweet remorse. The fatso feels some sense of accomplishment; this is no bunch of rumdums he forced into an error but a team with some class. We, the sinner's teammates, feel momentary anger at her – dumb! dumb play! – but then, seeing her grief, we sympathize with her in our hearts (any one of us might have made that mistake or one worse), and we yell encouragement, including the shortstop, who, moments before, dropped an easy throw for a force at second. 'That's all right! Come on! We got 'em!' we yell. 'Shake it off! These turkeys can't hit!' This makes us all feel good, even though the turkeys now lead us by ten runs. We're getting clobbered, but we have a winning attitude.

Let me say this about attitude: Each player is responsible for his or her own attitude, and to a considerable degree you can create a good attitude by doing certain little things on the field. These are certain little things that ballplayers do in the Bigs, and we ought to be doing them in the Slows.

1. When going up to bat, don't step right into the batter's box as if it were an elevator. The box is your turf, your stage. Take possession of it slowly and deliberately, starting with a lot of back-bending, knee-stretching, and torso-revolving in the on-deck circle. Then, approaching the box, stop outside it and tap the dirt off your spikes with your bat. You don't have spikes, you have sneakers, of course, but the significance of the tapping is the same. Then, upon entering the box, spit on the ground. It's a way of saying, 'This here is mine. This is where I get my hits.'

2. Spit frequently. Spit at all crucial moments. Spit correctly. Spit should be blown, not ptuied weakly with the lips, which often results in dribble. Spitting should convey forcefulness of purpose, concentration, pride. Spit down, not in the direction of others. Spit in the glove and on the fingers, especially after making a real knuck-lehead play; it's a way of saying, 'I dropped the ball because my glove was dry.'

3. At the bat and in the field, pick up dirt. Rub dirt in the fingers (especially after spitting on them). Toss dirt, as if testing the wind for velocity and direction. Smooth the dirt. Be involved with dirt. If no dirt is available (e.g. in the outfield), pluck tufts of grass. Fielders should be grooming their areas constantly between plays, flicking away tiny sticks and bits of gravel.

4. Take your time. Tie your laces. Confer with your teammates about possible options in dealing with them. Extend the game. Three errors on three consecutive plays can be humiliating if the plays occur within the space of a couple of minutes, but if each error is separated from the next by extensive conferences on the mound, lace-tying, glove adjustments, and arguing close calls (if any), the effect on morale is minimized.

5. Talk. Not just an occasional 'Let's get a hit now', but contin-uous rhythmic chatter, a flow of syllables: 'Hey babe hey babe c'mon babe good stick now hey be long tater take him downtown babe … hey good eye good eye.'

Infield chatter is harder to maintain. Since the slow-pitch pitch is required to be a soft underhand lob, infielders hesitate to say, 'Smoke him babe hey low heat hey; throw it on the black babe chuck it in there back him up babe no hit no hit.' Say it anyway.

6. One final rule, perhaps the most important of all: When your team has made the third out, the batter and the players who were left on base do not come back to the bench for their gloves. They remain on the field, and their teammates bring their gloves out to them. This requires some organization and discipline, but it pays off big in morale. It says, 'Although we're getting our pants knocked off, still we must conserve our energy.'

Imagine that you have bobbled two fly balls in this rout and now you have just tried to stretch a single into a double and have been easily thrown out sliding into second base, where the base runner ahead of you had stopped. It was the third out and a dumb play, and your opponents smirk at you as they run off the field. You are the goat, a lonely and tragic figure sitting in the dirt. You curse yourself, jerking your head sharply forward. You stand up and kick the base. How miserable! How degrading! Your utter shame, though brief, bears silent testimony to the worthiness of your team-mates, whom you have let down, and they appreciate it. They call out to you now as they take the field, and as the second baseman runs to his position he says, 'Let's get 'em now,' and tosses you your glove. Lowering your head, you trot slowly out to right. There you do some deep knee bends. You pick grass. You find a pebble and fling it into foul territory. As the first batter comes to the plate, you check the sun. You get set in your stance, poised to fly. Feet spread, hands on hips, you bend slightly at the waist and spit the expert spit of a veteran ballplayer – a player who has known the agony of defeat but who always bounces back, a player who has lost a stride on the base paths but can still make the big play.

This is *ball*, ladies and gentlemen. This is what it's all about.

WALTER THOM

From *Pedestrianism* (1813)

By the agreement, Capt. Barclay was to give Mr Fletcher eight days' notice of the day on which he was to start. The time was accordingly fixed for Tuesday the 10th of November; and the ground on which the bet was to be decided was the space of one mile on the high road between York and Hull, about sixteen miles from the former place. The contracting parties measured the ground, and a post was fixed at the end of the mile. In turning this post, it required a pace and a half additional each mile, which were not taken into the measurement. Persons were stationed at the winning post to notch down the rounds, and to observe that every thing was done in a fair manner. On each side of the road, a number of lamps were placed for the purpose of giving light during the darkness of the night. On Monday evening, Capt. Barclay appeared on the ground, accompanied by several of his friends, a few minutes before twelve o'clock; and Mr Fletcher also attended. Precisely at twelve, six stop watches were set, and put into a box at the winning end, which was sealed. At the same time, Capt. Barclay started. He was dressed in a flannel close shirt, flannel trowsers and night-cap, lambs'-wool stockings, and thick-soled leather shoes.

He went the two first miles in twenty-five minutes and ten seconds, and continued nearly at the same rate till he had gone sixteen miles, when he halted. The house into which he went to refresh was situated near the right side of the course, about ten yards from the road-side, which, in going and coming, made twenty yards, not included in the measurement. He remained about ten minutes in taking refreshment and changing clothes, when he proceeded with his match, went fifteen miles more, and then refreshed and changed as before.

At seven in the morning, which was rather hazy, Capt. Barclay appeared to be somewhat dull from the dampness of the night air. Betting, however, was two to one, and five to two in his favour. After refreshing, he was more cheerful, and went sixteen miles more, with much apparent strength, going each two miles in about twenty-five minutes and twenty seconds. By eleven, he had gone fifty miles, and appeared to proceed on his course with great ease and vigour. – Betting was now four and five to one in his favour.

When he had gone sixty miles, he stopped to refresh, and change clothes. He remained about ten minutes in the house, and came out in high spirits, with much cheerfulness in his countenance. Betting was now in his favour six and seven to one. He proceeded till he had gone seventy miles, scarcely varying in regularly performing each round of two miles in twenty-five minutes and a half, when he again refreshed and changed clothes. He appeared well and strong, and resumed his match in a gallant style.

He refreshed twice more, and performed the whole distance by twenty-two minutes four seconds past eight o'clock on Tuesday evening, being one hour, seven minutes, and fifty-six seconds within the specified time.

When he had finished, he was so strong and hearty, and in fact so well, that he could have continued for several hours longer, and might have gone twenty or thirty miles farther. – Thousands of spectators on foot and on horseback attended during the course of his walking, and he was loudly huzzahed, and carried on the shoulders of the multitude.

NORMAN GALE

The Church Cricketant (1894)

I bowled three sanctified souls
  With three consecutive balls!
What do I care if Blondin trod
  Over Niagara Falls?
What do I care for the loon in the Pit
  Or the gilded earl in the Stalls?
I bowled three curates once
  With three consecutive balls!

I caused three Protestant 'ducks'
  With three consecutive balls!
Poets may rave of lily girls
  Dancing in marble halls!
What do I care for a bevy of yachts,
  Or a dozen or so of yawls?
I bowled three curates once
  With three consecutive balls!

I bowled three cricketing priests
  With three consecutive balls!
What if a critic pounds a book,
  What if an author squalls?
What do I care if sciatica comes,
  Elephantiasis calls?
I bowled three curates once
  With three consecutive balls!

THOMAS HUGHES

From *Tom Brown's Schooldays* (1857)

As soon as dinner was over, and Tom had been questioned by such of his neighbours as were curious as to his birth, parentage, education, and other like matters, East, who evidently enjoyed his new dignity of patron and mentor, proposed having a look at the close, which Tom, athirst for knowledge, gladly assented to; and they went out through the quadrangle and past the big fives court, into the great playground.

'That's the chapel, you see,' said East; 'and there, just behind it, is the place for fights. You see it's most out of the way of the masters, who all live on the other side, and don't come by here after first lesson or callings-over. That's when the fights come off. And all this part where we are is the little-side ground, right up to the trees; and on the other side of the trees is the big-side ground, where the great matches are played. And there's the island in the farthest corner; you'll know that well enough next half, when there's island fagging. I say, it's horrid cold; let's have a run across.' And away went East, Tom close behind him. East was evidently putting his best foot foremost; and Tom, who was mighty proud of his running, and not a little anxious to show his friend that, although a new boy, he was no milksop, laid himself down to work in his very best style. Right across the close they went, each doing all he knew, and there wasn't a yard between them when they pulled up at the island moat.

'I say,' said East, as soon as he got his wind, looking with much increased respect at Tom, 'you ain't a bad scud, not by no means. Well, I'm as warm as a toast now.'

'But why do you wear white trousers in November?' said Tom. He had been struck by this peculiarity in the costume of almost all the School-house boys.

'Why, bless us, don't you know? No; I forgot. Why, today's the School-house match. Our house plays the whole of the School at football. And we all wear white trousers, to show 'em we don't care for hacks. You're in luck to come today. You just will see a match; and Brooke's going to let me play in quarters. That's more than he'll do for any other lower-school boy, except James, and he's fourteen.'

'Who's Brooke?'

'Why, that big fellow who called over at dinner, to be sure. He's cock of the school, and head of the School-house side, and the best kick and charger in Rugby.'

'Oh, but do show me where they play. And tell me about it. I love football so, and have played all my life. Won't Brooke let me play?'

'Not he,' said East, with some indignation. 'Why, you don't know the rules; you'll be a month learning them. And then it's no joke playing-up in a match, I can tell you − quite another thing from your private school games. Why, there's been two collar-bones broken this half, and a dozen fellows lamed. And last year a fellow had his leg broken.'

Tom listened with the profoundest respect to this chapter of accidents, and followed East across the level ground till they came to a sort of gigantic gallows of two poles, eighteen feet high, fixed upright in the ground some fourteen feet apart, with a cross-bar running from one to the other at the height of ten feet or thereabouts.

'This is one of the goals,' said East, 'and you see the other, across there, right opposite, under the Doctor's wall. Well, the match is for the best of three goals; whichever side kicks two goals wins: and it won't do, you see, just to kick the ball through these posts − it must go over the cross-bar; any height'll do, so long as it's between the posts. You'll have to stay in goal to touch the ball when it rolls behind the posts, because if the other side touch it they have a try at goal. Then we fellows in quarters, we play just about in front of goal here, and have to turn the ball and kick it back before the big fellows on the other side can follow it up. And in front of us all the big fellows play, and that's where the scrummages are mostly.'

Tom's respect increased as he struggled to make out his friend's technicalities, and the other set to work to explain the mysteries of 'off your side,' 'drop-kicks,' 'punts,' 'places,' and the other intricacies of the great science of football.

'But how do you keep the ball between the goals?' said he; 'I can't see why it mightn't go right down to the chapel.'

'Why; that's out of play,' answered East. 'You see this gravel-walk running down all along this side of the playing-ground, and the line of elms opposite on the other? Well, they're the bounds. As soon as the ball gets past them, it's in touch, and out of play. And then whoever first touches it has to knock it straight out amongst the players-up, who make two lines with a space between them, every fellow going on his own side. Ain't there just fine scrummages then! And the three trees you see there which come out into the play, that's a tremendous place when the ball hangs there, for you get thrown against the trees, and that's worse than any hack.'

Tom wondered within himself, as they strolled back again towards the fives court, whether the matches were really such break-neck affairs as East represented, and whether, if they were, he should ever get to like them and play up well.

He hadn't long to wonder, however, for next minute East cried out, 'Hurrah! Here's the punt-about; come along and try your hand at a kick.' The punt-about is the practice-ball, which is just brought out and kicked about anyhow from one boy to another before callings-over and dinner, and at other odd times. They joined the boys who had brought it out, all small School-house fellows, friends of East; and Tom had the pleasure of trying his skill, and performed very creditably, after first driving his foot three inches into the ground, and then nearly kicking his leg into the air, in vigorous efforts to accomplish a drop-kick after the manner of East.

Presently more boys and bigger came out, and boys from other houses on their way to calling-over, and more balls were sent for.

The crowd thickened as three o'clock approached; and when the hour struck, one hundred and fifty boys were hard at work. Then the balls were held, the master of the week came down in cap and gown to calling-over, and the whole school of three hundred boys swept into the big school to answer to their names.

'I may come in, mayn't I?' said Tom, catching East by the arm, and longing to feel one of them.

'Yes, come along; nobody'll say anything. You won't be so eager to get into calling-over after a month,' replied his friend; and they marched into the big school together, and up to the farther end, where that illustrious form, the lower fourth, which had the honour of East's patronage for the time being, stood.

The master mounted into the high desk by the door, and one of the prepostors of the week stood by him on the steps, the other three marching up and down the middle of the school with their canes, calling out, 'Silence, silence!' The sixth form stood close by the door on the left, some thirty in number, mostly great big grown men, as Tom thought, surveying them from a distance with awe; the fifth form behind them, twice their number, and not quite so big. These on the left; and on the right the lower fifth, shell, and all the junior forms in order; while up the middle marched the three prepostors.

Then the prepostor who stands by the master calls out the names, beginning with the sixth form; and as he calls each boy answers 'here' to his name, and walks out. Some of the sixth stop at the door to turn the whole string of boys into the close. It is a great match-day, and every boy in the school, will he, nill he, must be there. The rest of the sixth go forwards into the close, to see that no one escapes by any of the side gates.

Today, however, being the School-house match, none of the School-house prepostors stay by the door to watch for truants of their side; there is carte blanche to the School-house fags to go where they like. 'They trust to our honour,' as East proudly informs Tom; 'they know very well that no School-house boy would cut the match. If he did, we'd very soon cut him, I can tell you.'

The master of the week being short-sighted, and the prepostors of the week small and not well up to their work, the lower-school boys employ the ten minutes which elapse before their names are called in pelting one another vigorously with acorns, which fly about in all directions. The small prepostors dash in every now and then, and generally chastise some quiet, timid boy who is equally afraid of acorns and canes, while the principal performers get dexterously out of the way. And so calling-over rolls on somehow, much like the big world, punishments lighting on wrong shoulders, and matters going generally in a queer, cross-grained way, but the end coming somehow, which is, after all, the great point. And now the master of the week has finished, and locked up the big school; and the prepostors of the week come out, sweeping the last remnant of the school fags, who had been loafing about the corners by the fives court, in hopes of a chance of bolting, before them into the close.

'Hold the punt-about!' 'To the goals!' are the cries; and all stray balls are impounded by the authorities, and the whole mass of boys moves up towards the two goals, dividing as they go into three bodies. That little band on the left, consisting of from fifteen to twenty boys, Tom amongst them, who are making for the goal under the School-house wall, are the School-house boys who are not to play up, and have to stay in goal. The larger body moving to the island goal are the School boys in a like predicament. The great mass in the middle are the players-up, both sides mingled together; they are hanging their jackets (and all who mean real work), their hats, waistcoats, neck-handkerchiefs, and braces, on the railings round the small trees; and there they go by twos and threes up to their respective grounds. There is none of the colour and tastiness of get-up, you will perceive, which lends such a life to the present game at Rugby, making the dullest and worst-fought match a pretty sight. Now each house has its own uniform of cap and jersey, of some lively colour; but at the time we are speaking of plush caps have not yet come in, or uniforms of any sort, except the School-house white trousers, which are abominably cold today. Let us get to work, bare-headed, and girded with our plain leather straps. But we mean business, gentlemen.

And now that the two sides have fairly sundered, and each occupies its own ground, and we get a good look at them, what absurdity is this? You don't mean to say that those fifty or sixty boys in white trousers, many of them quite small, are going to play that huge mass opposite? Indeed I do, gentlemen. They're going to try, at any rate, and won't make such a bad fight of it either, mark my word; for hasn't old Brooke won the toss, with his lucky halfpenny, and got choice of goals and kick-off? The new ball you may see lie there quite by itself, in the middle, pointing towards the School or island goal; in another minute it will be well on its way there. Use that minute in remarking how the School-house side is drilled. You will see, in the first place, that the sixth-form boy, who has the charge of goal, has spread his force (the goalkeepers) so as to occupy the whole space behind the goal-posts, at distances of about five yards apart. A safe and well-kept goal is the foundation of all good play. Old Brooke is talking to the captain of quarters, and now he moves away. See how that youngster spreads his men (the light brigade) carefully over the ground, half-way between their own goal and the body of their own players-up (the heavy brigade). These again play in several bodies. There is young Brooke and the bull-dogs. Mark them well. They are the 'fighting brigade,' the 'die-hards,' larking about at leap-frog to keep themselves warm, and playing tricks on one another. And on each side of old Brooke, who is now standing in the middle of the ground and just going to kick off, you see a separate wing of players-up, each with a boy of acknowledged prowess to look to – here Warner, and there Hedge; but over all is old Brooke, absolute as he of Russia, but wisely and bravely ruling over willing and worshipping subjects, a true football king. His face is earnest and careful as he glances a last time over his array, but full of pluck and hope – the sort of look I hope to see in my general when I go out to fight.

The School side is not organized in the same way. The goal-keepers are all in lumps, anyhow and nohow; you can't distinguish between the players-up and the boys in quarters, and there is divided leadership. But with such odds in strength and weight it must take more than that to hinder them from winning; and so their leaders seem to think, for they let the players-up manage themselves.

But now look! There is a slight move forward of the School-house wings, a shout of 'Are you ready?' and loud affirmative reply. Old Brooke takes half a dozen quick steps, and away goes the ball spinning towards the School goal, seventy yards before it touches ground, and at no point above twelve or fifteen feet high, a model kick-off; and the School-house cheer and rush on. The ball is returned, and they meet it and drive it back amongst the masses of the School already in motion. Then the two sides close, and you can see nothing for minutes but a swaying crowd of boys, at one point violently agitated. That is where the ball is, and there are the keen players to be met, and the glory and the hard knocks to be got. You hear the dull thud, thud of the ball, and the shouts of 'Off your side,' 'Down with him,' 'Put him over,' 'Bravo.' This is what we call 'a scrummage,' gentlemen, and the first scrummage in a School-house match was no joke in the consulship of Plancus.

But see! It has broken; the ball is driven out on the School-house side, and a rush of the School carries it past the School-house players-up. 'Look out in quarters,' Brooke's and twenty other voices ring out. No need to call, though: the School-house captain of quarters has caught it on the bound, dodges the foremost School boys, who are heading the rush, and sends it back with a good drop-kick well into the enemy's country. And then follows rush upon rush, and scrummage upon scrummage, the ball now driven through into the School-house quarters, and now into the School goal; for the School-house have not lost the advantage which the kick-off and a slight wind gave them at the outset, and are slightly 'penning' their adversaries. You say you don't see much in it all – nothing but a struggling mass of boys, and a leather ball which seems to excite them all to great fury, as a red rag does a bull. My dear sir, a battle would look much the same to you, except that the boys would be men, and the balls iron; but a battle would be worth your looking at for all that, and so is a football match. You can't be expected to appreciate the delicate strokes of play, the turns by which a game is lost and won – it takes an old player to do that; but the broad philosophy of football you can understand if you will. Come along with me a little nearer, and let us consider it together.

The ball has just fallen again where the two sides are thickest, and they close rapidly around it in a scrummage. It must be driven through now by force or skill, till it flies out on one side or the other. Look how differently the boys face it! Here come two of the bulldogs, bursting through the outsiders; in they go, straight to the heart of the scrummage, bent on driving that ball out on the opposite side. That is what they mean to do. My sons, my sons! You are too hot; you have gone past the ball, and must struggle now right through the scrummage, and get round and back again to your own side, before you can be of any further use. Here comes young Brooke; he goes in as straight as you, but keeps his head, and backs and bends, holding himself still behind the ball, and driving it furiously when he gets the chance. Take a leaf out of his book, you young chargers. Here comes Speedicut, and Flashman the School-house bully, with shouts and great action. Won't you two come up to young Brooke, after locking-up, by the School-house fire, with 'Old fellow, wasn't that just a splendid scrummage by the three trees?' But he knows you, and so do we. You don't really want to drive that ball through that scrummage, chancing all hurt for the glory of the School-house, but to make us think that's what you want – a vastly different thing; and fellows of your kidney will never go through more than the skirts of a scrummage, where it's all push and no kicking. We respect boys who keep out of it, and don't sham going in; but you – we had rather not say what we think of you.

Then the boys who are bending and watching on the outside, mark them: they are most useful players, the dodgers, who seize on the ball the moment it rolls out from amongst the chargers, and away with it across to the opposite goal. They seldom go into the scrummage, but must have more coolness than the chargers. As endless as are boys' characters, so are their ways of facing or not facing a scrummage at football.

Three-quarters of an hour are gone; first winds are failing, and weight and numbers beginning to tell. Yard by yard the School-house have been driven back, contesting every inch of ground. The bull-dogs are the colour of mother earth from shoulder to ankle, except young Brooke, who has a marvellous knack of keeping his legs. The School-house are being penned in their turn, and now the ball is behind their goal, under the Doctor's wall. The Doctor and some of his family are there looking on, and seem as anxious as any boy for the success of the School-house. We get a minute's breathing-time before old Brooke kicks out, and he gives the word to play strongly for touch, by the three trees. Away goes the ball, and the bull-dogs after it, and in another minute there is shout of 'In touch!' 'Our ball!' Now's your time, old Brooke, while your men are still fresh. He stands with the ball in his hand, while the two sides form in deep lines opposite one another; he must strike it straight out between them. The lines are thickest close to him, but young Brooke and two or three of his men are shifting up farther, where the opposite line is weak. Old Brooke strikes it out straight and strong, and it falls opposite his brother. Hurrah! That rush has taken it right through the School line, and away past the three trees, far into their quarters, and young Brooke and the bull-dogs are close upon it. The School leaders rush back, shouting, 'Look out in goal!' and strain every nerve to catch him, but they are after the fleetest foot in Rugby. There they go straight for the School goal-posts, quarters scattering before them. One after another the bull-dogs go down, but young Brooke holds on. 'He is down.' No! A long stagger, but the danger is past. That was the shock of Crew, the most dangerous of dodgers. And now he is close to the School goal, the ball not three yards before him. There is a hurried rush of the School fags to the spot, but no one throws himself on the ball, the only chance, and young Brooke has touched it right under the School goal-posts.

The School leaders come up furious, and administer toco to the wretched fags nearest at hand. They may well be angry, for it is all Lombard Street to a china orange that the School-house kick a goal with the ball touched in such a good place. Old Brooke, of course, will kick it out, but who shall catch and place it? Call Crab Jones.

Here he comes, sauntering along with a straw in his mouth, the queerest, coolest fish in Rugby. If he were tumbled into the moon this minute, he would just pick himself up without taking his hands out of his pockets or turning a hair. But it is a moment when the boldest charger's heart beats quick. Old Brooke stands with the ball under his arm motioning the School back; he will not kick out till they are all in goal, behind the posts. They are all edging forwards, inch by inch, to get nearer for the rush at Crab Jones, who stands there in front of old Brooke to catch the ball. If they can reach and destroy him before he catches, the danger is over; and with one and the same rush they will carry it right away to the School-house goal. Fond hope! It is kicked out and caught beautifully. Crab strikes his heel into the ground, to mark the spot where the ball was caught, beyond which the school line may not advance; but there they stand, five deep, ready to rush the moment the ball touches the ground. Take plenty of room. Don't give the rush a chance of reaching you. Place it true and steady. Trust Crab Jones. He has made a small hole with his heel for the ball to lie on, by which he is resting on one knee, with his eye on old Brooke. 'Now!' Crab places the ball at the word, old Brooke kicks, and it rises slowly and truly as the School rush forward.

Then a moment's pause, while both sides look up at the spinning ball. There it flies, straight between the two posts, some five feet above the cross-bar, an unquestioned goal; and a shout of real, genuine joy rings out from the School-house players-up, and a faint echo of it comes over the close from the goal-keepers under the Doctor's wall. A goal in the first hour – such a thing hasn't been done in the School-house match these five years.

'Over!' is the cry. The two sides change goals, and the School-house goal-keepers come threading their way across through the masses of the School, the most openly triumphant of them – amongst whom is Tom, a School-house boy of two hours' standing – getting their ears boxed in the transit. Tom indeed is excited beyond measure, and it is all the sixth-form boy, kindest and safest of goal-keepers, has been able to do, to keep him from rushing out whenever the ball has been near their goal. So he holds him by his side, and instructs him in the science of touching.

At this moment Griffith, the itinerant vender of oranges from Hill Morton, enters the close with his heavy baskets. There is a rush of small boys upon the little pale-faced man, the two sides mingling together, subdued by the great goddess Thirst, like the English and French by the streams in the Pyrenees. The leaders are past oranges and apples, but some of them visit their coats, and apply innocent-looking ginger-beer bottles to their mouths. It is no ginger-beer though, I fear, and will do you no good. One short mad rush, and then a stitch in the side, and no more honest play. That's what comes of those bottles.

But now Griffith's baskets are empty, the ball is placed again midway, and the School are going to kick off. Their leaders have sent their lumber into goal, and rated the rest soundly, and one hundred and twenty picked players-up are there, bent on retrieving the game. They are to keep the ball in front of the School-house goal, and then to drive it in by sheer strength and weight. They mean heavy play and no mistake, and so old Brooke sees, and places Crab Jones in quarters just before the goal, with four or five picked players who are to keep the ball away to the sides, where a try at goal, if obtained, will be less dangerous than in front. He himself, and Warner and Hedge, who have saved themselves till now, will lead the charges.

'Are you ready?' 'Yes.' And away comes the ball, kicked high in the air, to give the School time to rush on and catch it as it falls. And here they are amongst us. Meet them like Englishmen, you School-house boys, and charge them home. Now is the time to show what mettle is in you; and there shall be a warm seat by the hall fire, and honour, and lots of bottled beer to-night for him who does his duty in the next half-hour.

And they are well met. Again and again the cloud of their players-up gathers before our goal, and comes threatening on, and Warner or Hedge, with young Brooke and the relics of the bull-dogs, break through and carry the ball back; and old Brooke ranges the field like Job's war-horse. The thickest scrummage parts asunder before his rush, like the waves before a clipper's bows; his cheery voice rings out over the field, and his eye is everywhere. And if these miss the ball, and it rolls dangerously in front of our goal, Crab Jones and his men have seized it and sent it away towards the sides with the unerring drop-kick. This is worth living for – the whole sum of school-boy existence gathered up into one straining, struggling half-hour, a half-hour worth a year of common life.

The quarter to five has struck, and the play slackens for a minute before goal; but there is Crew, the artful dodger, driving the ball in behind our goal, on the island side, where our quarters are weakest. Is there no one to meet him? Yes; look at little East! The ball is just at equal distances between the two, and they rush together, the young man of seventeen and the boy of twelve, and kick it at the same moment. Crew passes on without a stagger; East is hurled forward by the shock, and plunges on his shoulder, as if he would bury himself in the ground; but the ball rises straight into the air, and falls behind Crew's back, while the 'bravoes' of the School-house attest the pluckiest charge of all that hard-fought day. Warner picks East up lame and half stunned, and he hobbles back into goal, conscious of having played the man.

And now the last minutes are come, and the School gather for their last rush, every boy of the hundred and twenty who has a run left in him. Reckless of the defence of their own goal, on they come across the level big-side ground, the ball well down amongst them, straight for our goal, like the column of the Old Guard up the slope at Waterloo. All former charges have been child's play to this. Warner and Hedge have met them, but still on they come. The bull-dogs rush in for the last time; they are hurled over or carried back, striving hand, foot, and eyelids. Old Brooke comes sweeping round the skirts of the play, and turning short round, picks out the very heart of the scrummage, and plunges in. It wavers for a moment; he has the ball. No, it has passed him, and his voice rings out clear over the advancing tide, 'Look out in goal!' Crab Jones catches it for a moment; but before he can kick, the rush is upon him and passes over him; and he picks himself up behind them with his straw in his mouth, a little dirtier, but as cool as ever.

The ball rolls slowly in behind the School-house goal, not three yards in front of a dozen of the biggest School players-up.

There stands the School-house prepostor, safest of goal-keepers, and Tom Brown by his side, who has learned his trade by this time. Now is your time, Tom. The blood of all the Browns is up, and the two rush in together, and throw themselves on the ball, under the very feet of the advancing column – the prepostor on his hands and knees, arching his back, and Tom all along on his face. Over them topple the leaders of the rush, shooting over the back of the prepostor, but falling flat on Tom, and knocking all the wind out of his small carcass. 'Our ball,' says the prepostor, rising with his prize; 'but get up there; there's a little fellow under you.' They are hauled and roll off him, and Tom is discovered, a motionless body.

Old Brooke picks him up. 'Stand back, give him air,' he says; and then feeling his limbs, adds, 'No bones broken. – How do you feel, young un?'

'Hah-hah!' gasps Tom, as his wind comes back; 'pretty well, thank you – all right.'

'Who is he?' says Brooke.

'Oh, it's Brown; he's a new boy; I know him,' says East, coming up.

'Well, he is a plucky youngster, and will make a player,' says Brooke.

And five o'clock strikes. 'No side' is called, and the first day of the School-house match is over.

DAVID STOREY

From *This Sporting Life* (1960)

At Thursday night training I was told George Wade wouldn't be travelling on Saturday with the first team to Wakefield, but was saving himself the journey and watching the 'A' team. I took this to mean he was watching me, though there were four other trialists in the team. In the changing room before the match I acted like the Big Frog around the place. I rubbed on other people's vaseline, tied other people's shoulder pads and bandages, did a lot of shadow boxing in the corner. There was no doubt what I was aiming for. And for the first time the weather was fine.

I heard my name go out over the loudspeaker, then the roar of the crowd as the visiting team went out first. Dicky, the trainer, gave us his last instructions, we lined up, and moved down the tunnel. The front of the line broke into a trot. The boots clacked on the concrete, then slurred and were suddenly silent as they prodded into the bare earth just inside the tunnel mouth.

The darkness broke away. The light blinded for a second, mingled with the shock of the crowd's roar. I seemed to inflate as I ran on to the field. The loudspeakers blared 'The Entrance of the Gladiators' as we ran quickly, importantly, to the middle of the field, and swerved aside to make a circle. The tune changed to a crackly fanfare as the captains tossed up. The teams spread out, filtered across the pitch, and stood still, red and blue in the worn brown and dusty green patches of the field. We waited, quiet, for the whistle. It blasted. The ball rose into the air.

Fifteen minutes of the first half passed and I'd never even touched the ball. I was aching with activity, and blowing hard. It took me most of the first half to realize I was being starved of the ball by my own team.

It was the hooker, Taff Gower, who was organizing it, I decided; a quiet little frog working out his last days in the game with the 'A' team. With his scarred, toothless face, his short bow-legged figure stumped alongside me in each movement and casually diverted the ball whenever it came my way. I gathered he mustn't like me. I might be keeping one of his mates out of the team, stopping a wage. I didn't worry about this. I just saw an early end to my ambitions. As we folded down for the next scrum his face was further forward than mine. 'Why're you keeping the ball from me?' I asked him. His head was upside down, waiting for the ball to come in, but he was grinning, fairly politely. I could see the back of his throat. When he spat I couldn't move my head. I didn't think he could like me.

I waited three scrums, to make him feel relaxed and also to get the best opportunity. I kept my right arm loose. His face was upside down, his eyes straining, loose in their sockets, to catch a glimpse of the ball as it came in. I watched it leave the scrum-half's hands and his head buckled under the forwards' heaving. I swung my right fist into the middle of his face. He cried out loud. I hit him again and saw the red pulp of his nose and lips as my hand came away. He was crying out really loud now, partly affected, professional pain, but most of it real. His language echoed all over the ground.

The scrum broke up with the ref blowing his nut off on the whistle. 'I saw that! I saw that!' he shouted, urged on to violent mimes of justice by the crowd's tremendous booing. They were all on their feet demonstrating and screaming. Gower had covered his face with his hands, but blood seeped between his fingers, as the trainer and two players directed his blind steps off the field.

'You'll be nailed for good for this, you dirty little swine. You'll never play again,' and all that, the ref was shouting. He pointed with real drama at the opposing hooker. The crowd's response reached a crescendo – far more than it would provide for, say, the burning of a church.

The young hooker shook his head. 'I ne'er touched him,' he said, looking round for support from his own team. 'I swear to God I never touched him.'

'You can tell that to the league chairman!'

The hooker was beside himself with innocence. 'Nay, look at my bloody fist,' he said. 'Look, there's no blood on it.'

'I'm not arguing.'

The ref took his name and sent him off.

I'd never seen such a parade before. The whole ground throbbed with rage as the young figure in his little boy's costume passed in front of the main stand.

'They're not fit to be on a football field,' the ref said to me, since I happened to be standing nearest. I didn't know whether he meant the crowd or men like the hooker. The free kick put us two points ahead.

We stood around the tunnel mouth at half-time, drinking from the bottles and listening to Dicky tell us a few yards of mistakes. We were quiet. It was a fact that since Gower had gone off I'd been getting the ball just as I liked it, and as often as not in openings. I was looking up, trying to pick George Wade's homburg out in the committee box, when Dicky came over to me. He took hold of my hand and looked at the knuckles.

'Got some nice bruises there, owd lad,' he said. 'What got into you?' He didn't look at me, but at the other players.

'How d'you mean?'

'Taff Gower – you could see it plain as day from the bench.'

'He was keeping the ball from me.'

'Come off it, owd cock. Nobody lakes that game here.'

'Not now they don't.'

He grimaced, annoyed I should try to be smart. 'You'll do just fine at this club,' he said. 'Any rate, I'm not saying a word about it, 'less Wade asks me in private.'

'You're on my side,' I told him.

'Get this, lad. I'm on my own side.' He winked, importantly, and banged my shoulder. 'Keep it up, Art,' he said in a loud voice, and went over to advise the full-back.

As we stood on the field waiting for the second half kick-off, I examined everything with real care, telling myself I ought to savour every second of this feeling. I had my eyes fixed on the twin buds of the power station's cooling towers, and watched a cloud of white steam escape across the valley and come over the pitch. The ball rose towards it, and in a slow curve fell towards me. I gathered it cleanly and, beating two men, ran to the centre of the field. Somebody shouted for the ball. I kept it. I found myself in an opening and suddenly thought I might even reach the line. I went straight for the full-back, and when he came in I gave him the base of my wrist on his nose. The crack, the groan, the release of his arms, all coincided with a soaring of my guts. I moved in between the posts keeping my eye on the delight of the crowd as I put the ball down.

Everything was luminous, sparkling. The houses beyond the stadium turrets, the silhouetted trees at Sandwood, the iceblue sky, the mass of people – they were all there intent on seeing me. I was carried along in a bag full of energy, no longer aware of effort, ready to tear anybody into postage stamps and at the same time smile for the crowd. I came off the field fresher than when I went on, and still waiting for some damn thing to tire me.

Although George Wade wasn't in the tearoom, Johnson was. He devoured me with a rapturous gaze and slipped his little arm round me, swaying and chanting, and bringing a lot of eyes in our direction. 'What a game, Arthur! What a blind!' He talked so much wind I'd to take him to the bar to try and quieten him down. He immediately danced off to the lavatory: he'd been holding himself till he saw me. I ordered two beers.

'Allow me,' a voice said over my shoulder. I turned round to see the soft features of a smiling face. 'No, allow me. I really do insist,' the man went on, and although I wasn't supposed to know I knew this was Weaver. He held my money away from the barman and slid a quid note in its place. He took off his hat and ordered a beer for himself.

'You had a good game today, Arthur,' he said, intimately, as if we were good friends. 'How do you like the City?' His little protruding lips parted to small, even teeth, which weren't, yet looked, artificial.

'It's my third game. It's going all right, I reckon.'

'Yes,' he said. 'So I gathered. You seem to have made a good start. If you don't mind me saying so.' He nodded towards the frosted glass of the committee room. 'Wade's been talking about you in there. I imagine it was just the day for it.' He nodded this time to the window overlooking the pitch. 'Do you like a firm going?'

'I must do.'

He laughed extravagantly. I saw Johnson emerge from the lavatory and stand some distance away. I beckoned to him but he didn't come.

'Have you played for any other club ... any of the Intermediate League?' Weaver asked, and took no notice of my attempt to attract Johnson. I shook my head.

'I didn't think I'd heard your name before – Machin.' He made it sound fairly common. We stared at one another with an instinctive sort of reaction. 'It's a great pity about Taffy Gower.'

'What's happened? I didn't see him after the match.'

'You wouldn't. They've taken him for an X-ray. Gone to hospital. I heard it was a broken nose. For a little fellow ... their hooker's got quite a punch.' He was smiling, almost laughing, and blinking his blue eyes.

'Bad luck.'

'It is.' He picked up his hat and left his beer undrunk. 'I better be pushing along. You're not signed on here, yet?' 'I've another game before they make up their minds.'

'I don't think they'll have much difficulty there, do you?' He blinked his baby eyes again, folding them up in those fleshy encasements. 'Bye, Arthur.'

As soon as he'd gone, I turned to Johnson.

'Who was it?' I asked him.

'You should know, Arthur.' He knew I knew.

'Who was it?'

'Guess… Go on, have a guess.' The grin on his face showed he was enjoying the game.

5

SPORT AND LIFE

Sport fits easily into the role of being a metaphor for actual life, but these passages have been selected to propose that the relationship between sport and life is rather more complex.

Ascham's book on archery, Toxophilus, *is in the form of a dialogue between Philologus (Lover of study) and Toxophilus (Lover of the bow), in which the conversation uses sport to draw out an understanding of life. In this excerpt they discuss fencing, including the inevitability of failure — while nobody can hit the mark every time, the possibility that it can be done leads us to strive towards that goal. John Donne's goal is clear from line one, but he delights in playing with the words; the poem pitches Donne and his intended both as lovers and as bait and fish.*

Bennett's The Matador of the Five Towns *and Sillitoe's* The Loneliness of the Long Distance Runner *explore the violence latent in sport — the potential to wreck hope and expectation as well as bodies. Sport as destruction is the theme here, self-destruction and destruction of the other, the Saturday afternoon adversary of the football match and the permanent enemy of authority.*

Blake's 'The Ecchoing Green' from Songs of Innocence *is a challenge to the aggression of these stories; its place is to offer an alternative, where 'sport' means 'play'. But there is melancholy here too, and what binds the watching grandparent and the 'potential homicides' on the football terraces is the knowledge that they are spectators rather than performers. The 'Curlers' Grace' takes all this in its stride, in the security of both the team and a higher providence.*

But we begin with Henry Newbolt's imperial analogy, frequently looked down on but as impossible to ignore as a Curtly Ambrose bouncer.

SIR HENRY NEWBOLT

Vitaï Lampada (1892)

There's a breathless hush in the Close to-night –
Ten to make and the match to win –
A bumping pitch and a blinding light,
An hour to play and the last man in.
And it's not for the sake of a ribboned coat,
Or the selfish hope of a season's fame,
But his Captain's hand on his shoulder smote
'Play up! play up! and play the game!'

The sand of the desert is sodden red –
Red with the wreck of a square that broke –
The Gatling's jammed and the colonel dead,
And the regiment blind with dust and smoke.
The river of death has brimmed his banks,
And England's far, and Honour a name,
But the voice of schoolboy rallies the ranks,
'Play up! play up! and play the game!'

This is the word that year by year
While in her place the School is set
Every one of her sons must hear,
And none that hears it dare forget.
This they all with a joyful mind
Bear through life like a torch in flame,
And falling fling to the host behind –
'Play up! play up! and play the game!'

ALAN SILLITOE

From *The Loneliness of the Long Distance Runner* (1959)

Now I can hear the sportsground noise and music as I head back for the flags and the lead-in drive, the fresh new feel of underfoot gravel going against the iron muscles of my legs. I'm nowhere near puffed despite that bag of nails that rattles as much as ever, and I can still give a big last leap like gale-force wind if I want to, but everything is under control and I know now that there ain't another long-distance cross-country running runner in England to touch my speed and style. Our doddering bastard of a governor, our half-dead gangrened gaffer is hollow like an empty petrol drum, and he wants me and my running life to give him glory, to put in him blood and thobbing veins he never had, wants his potbellied pals to be his witnesses as I gasp and stagger up to his winning post so's he can say: 'My Borstal gets that cup, you see. I win my bet, because it pays to be honest and try to gain the prizes I offer to my lads, and they know it, have known it all along. They'll always be honest now, because I made them so.' And his pals will think: 'He trains his lads to live right, after all; he deserves a medal but we'll get him made a Sir' – and at this very moment as the birds come back to whistling I can tell myself I'll never care a sod what any of the chinless spine-less in-laws think or say. They've seen me and they're cheering now and loudspeakers set around the field like elephant's ears are spreading out the big news that I'm well in the lead, and can't do anything else but stay there. But I'm still thinking of the out-law death my dad died, telling the doctors to scat from the house when they wanted him to finish up in hospital (like a bleeding guinea-pig, he raved at them). He got up in bed to throw them out and even followed them down the stairs in his shirt though he was no more than skin and stick. They tried to tell him he'd want some drugs but he didn't fall for it, and only took the pain-killer that mam and I got from a herbseller in the next street. It's not till now that I know what guts he had, and when I went into the room that morning he was lying on his stomach with the clothes thrown back, looking like a skinned rabbit, his grey head resting just on the edge of the bed, and on the floor must have been all the blood he'd had in his body, right from his toe-nails up, for nearly all of the lino and carpet was covered in it, thin and pink.

And down the drive I went, carrying a heart blocked up like Boulder Dam across my arteries, the nail-bag clamped down tighter and tighter as though in a woodwork vice, yet with my feet like birdwings and arms like talons ready to fly across the field except that I didn't want to give anybody that much of a show, or win the race by accident. I smell the hot dry day now as I run towards the end, passing a mountain-heap of grass emptied from cans hooked on to the fronts of lawnmowers pushed by my pals; I rip a piece of tree-bark with my fingers and stuff it in my mouth, chewing wood and dust and maybe maggots as I run until I'm nearly sick, yet swallowing what I can of it just the same because a little birdie whistled to me that I've got to go on living for at least a bloody sight longer yet but that for six months I'm not going to smell that grass or taste that dusty bark or trot this lovely path. I hate to have to say this but something bloody-well made me cry, and crying is a thing I haven't bloody-well done since I was a kid of two or three. Because I'm slowing down now for Gunthorpe to catch me up, and I'm doing it in a place just where the drive turns in to the sportsfield – where they can see what I'm doing, especially the governor and his gang from the grandstand, and I'm going so slow I'm almost marking time. Those on the nearest seats haven't caught on yet to what's happening and are still cheering like mad ready for when I make that mark, and I keep on wondering when the bleeding hell Gunthorpe behind me is going to nip by on the field because I can't hold this up all day, and I think Oh Christ it's just my rotten luck that Gunthorpe's dropped out and that I'll be here for half an hour before the next bloke comes up, but even so, I say, I won't budge, I won't go for that last hundred yards if I have to sit down cross-legged on the grass and have the governor and his chinless wonders pick me up and carry me there, which is against their rules so you can bet they'd never do it because they're not clever enough to break the rules – like I would be in their place – even though they are their own. No, I'll show him what honesty means if it's the last thing I do, though I'm sure he'll never understand because if he and all them like him did it'd mean they'd be on my side which is impossible. By God I'll stick this out like my dad stuck out his pain and kicked them doctors down the stairs: if he had guts for that then I've got guts for this and here I stay waiting for Gunthorpe or Aylesham to bash that turf and go right slap-up against that bit of clothes-line stretched across the winning post. As for me, the only time I'll hit that clothes-line will be when I'm dead and a comfortable coffin's been got ready on the other side. Until then I'm a long-distance runner, crossing country all on my own no matter how bad it feels.

The Essex boys were shouting themselves blue in the face telling me to get a move on, waving their arms, standing up and making as if to run at that rope themselves because they were only a few yards to the side of it. You cranky lot, I thought, stuck at that winning post, and yet I knew they didn't mean what they were shouting, were really on my side and always would be, not able to keep their maulers to themselves, in and out of cop-shops and clink. And there they were now having the time of their lives letting themselves go in cheering me which made the governor think they were heart and soul on his side when he wouldn't have thought any such thing if he'd had a grain of sense. And I could hear the lords and ladies now from the grandstand, and could see them standing up to wave me in: 'Run!' they were shouting in their posh voices. 'Run!'

But I was deaf, daft and blind, and stood where I was, still tasting the bark in my mouth and still blubbing like a baby, blubbing now out of gladness that I'd got them beat at last.

ROGER ASCHAM

From *Toxophilus* (1545)

But in learning of fence, I pray you what is that which men most labour for?

Toxophilus. That they may hit another, I trow, and never take blow their self.

Philologus. You say truth, and I am sure every one of them would fain do so whensoever he playeth. But was there ever any of them so cunning yet, which, at one time or other, hath not been touched.

Tox. The best of them all is glad sometime to escape with a blow.

Phi. Then in fence also, men are taught to go about that thing, which the best of them all knoweth he shall never attain unto. Moreover you that be shooters, I pray you, what mean you, when ye take so great heed to keep your standing, to shoot compass, to look on your mark so diligently, to cast up grass divers times, and other things more you know better than I. What would you do then, I pray you?

Tox. Hit the mark if we could.

Phi. And doth every man go about to hit the mark at every shot?

Tox. By my troth I trow so; and, as for myself, I am sure I do.

Phi. But all men do not hit it at all times.

Tox. No, truly, for that were a wonder.

Phi. Can any man hit it at all times?

Tox. No man, verily.

Phi. Then belikely, to hit the prick always is impossible. For that is called impossible which is in no man his power to do.

Tox. Unpossible indeed.

Phi. But to shoot wide and far of the mark is a thing possible.

Tox. No man will deny that.

Phi. But yet to hit the mark always were an excellent thing.

Tox. Excellent, surely.

Phi. Then I am sure those be wiser men which covet to shoot wide, than those which covet to hit the prick.

Tox. Why so, I pray you?

Phi. Because to shoot wide is a thing possible, and therefore, as you say yourself, of every wise man to be followed. And as for hitting the prick, because it is impossible, it were a vain thing to go about it in good sadness, Toxophile; thus you see that a man might go through all crafts and sciences, and prove that any man in his science coveteth that which he shall never get.

Tox. By my troth (as you say) I cannot deny but they do so; but why and wherefore they should do so, I cannot learn.

Phi. I will tell you. Every craft and science standeth in two things: in knowing of his craft, and working of his craft; for perfect knowledge bringeth a man to perfect working: this know painters, carvers, tailors, shoemakers, and all other craftsmen, to be true.

JOHN DONNE

The Bait (1633)

Come live with me, and be my love,
And we will some new pleasures prove
Of golden sands, and crystal brooks,
With silken lines, and silver hooks.

There will the river whispering run
Warm'd by thy eyes, more than the sun;
And there the 'enamour'd fish will stay,
Begging themselves they may betray.

When thou wilt swim in that live bath,
Each fish, which every channel hath,
Will amorously to thee swim,
Gladder to catch thee, than thou him.

If thou, to be so seen, be'st loth,
By sun or moon, thou dark'nest both,
And if myself have leave to see,
I need not their light having thee.

Let others freeze with angling reeds,
And cut their legs with shells and weeds,
Or treacherously poor fish beset,
With strangling snare, or windowy net.

Let coarse bold hands from slimy nest
The bedded fish in banks out-wrest;
Or curious traitors, sleeve-silk flies,
Bewitch poor fishes' wand'ring eyes.

For thee, thou need'st no such deceit,
For thou thyself art thine own bait:
That fish, that is not catch'd thereby,
Alas, is wiser far than I.

WILLIAM BLAKE

The Ecchoing Green (1789)

The sun does arise,
And make happy the skies.
The merry bells ring
To welcome the Spring.
The sky-lark and thrush,
The birds of the bush,
Sing louder around,
To the bells' cheerful sound.
While our sports shall be seen
On the Ecchoing Green.

Old John, with white hair
Does laugh away care,
Sitting under the oak,
Among the old folk,
They laugh at our play,
And soon they all say.
'Such, such were the joys.
When we all girls & boys,
In our youth-time were seen,
On the Ecchoing Green.'

Till the little ones weary
No more can be merry
The sun does descend,
And our sports have an end:
Round the laps of their mothers,
Many sisters and brothers,

Like birds in their nest,
Are ready for rest;
And sport no more seen,
On the darkening Green.

ARNOLD BENNETT

From *The Matador of Five Towns* (1912)

We went on the Grand Stand, which was packed with men whose eyes were fixed, with an unconscious but intense effort, on a common object. Among the men were a few women in furs and wraps, equally absorbed. Nobody took any notice of us as we insinuated our way up a rickety flight of wooden stairs, but when by misadventure we grazed a human being the elbow of that being shoved itself automatically and fiercely outwards, to repel. I had an impression of hats, caps, and woolly overcoats stretched in long parallel lines, and of grimy raw planks everywhere presenting possibly dangerous splinters, save where use had worn them into smooth shininess. Then gradually I became aware of the vast field, which was more brown than green. Around the field was a wide border of infinitesimal hats and pale faces, rising in tiers, and beyond this border fences, hoardings, chimneys, furnaces, gasometers, telegraph-poles, houses, and dead trees. And here and there, perched in strange perilous places, even high up towards the sombre sky, were more human beings clinging. On the field itself, at one end of it, were a scattered handful of doll-like figures, motionless; some had white bodies, others red; and three were in black; all were so small and so far off that they seemed to be mere unimportant casual incidents in whatever recondite affair it was that was proceeding. Then a whistle shrieked, and all these figures began simultaneously to move, and then I saw a ball in the air. An obscure, uneasy murmuring rose from the immense multitude like an invisible but audible vapour. The next instant the vapour had condensed into a sudden shout. Now I saw the ball rolling solitary in the middle of the field, and a single red doll racing towards it; at one end was a confused group of red and white, and at the other two white dolls, rather lonely in the expanse. The single red doll overtook the ball and scudded along with it at his twinkling toes. A great voice behind me bellowed with an incredible volume of sound:

'Now, Jos!'

And another voice, further away, bellowed:

'Now, Jos!'

And still more distantly the grim warning shot forth from the crowd:

'Now, Jos! Now, Jos!'

The nearer of the white dolls, as the red one approached, sprang forward. I could see a leg. And the ball was flying back in a magnificent curve into the skies; it passed out of my sight, and then I heard a bump on the slates of the roof of the grandstand, and it fell among the crowd in the stand-enclosure. But almost before the flight of the ball had commenced, a terrific roar of relief had rolled formidably round the field, and out of that roar, like rockets out of thick smoke, burst acutely ecstatic cries of adoration:

'Bravo, Jos!'

'Good old Jos!'

The leg had evidently been Jos's leg. The nearer of these two white dolls must be Jos, darling of fifteen thousand frenzied people.

Stirling punched a neighbour in the side to attract his attention.

'What's the score?' he demanded of the neighbour, who scowled and then grinned.

'Two – one – agen uz!' The other growled.

'It'll take our b – s all their time to draw. They're playing a man short.'

'Accident?'

'No! Referee ordered him off for rough play.'

Several spectators began to explain, passionately, furiously, that the referee's action was utterly bereft of common sense and justice. I gathered that a less gentlemanly crowd would undoubtedly have lynched the referee. The explanations died down, and everybody except me resumed his fierce watch on the field.

I was recalled from the exercise of a vague curiosity upon the set, anxious faces around me by a crashing, whooping cheer which in volume and sincerity of joy surpassed all noises in my experience. This massive cheer reverberated round the field like the echoes of a battleship's broadside in a fiord. But it was human, and therefore more terrible than guns. I instinctively thought: 'If such are the symptoms of pleasure, what must be the symptoms of pain or disappointment?' Simultaneously with the expulsion of the unique noise the expression of the faces changed. Eyes sparkled; teeth became prominent in enormous, uncontrolled smiles. Ferocious satisfaction had to find vent in ferocious gestures, wreaked either upon dead wood or upon the living tissues of fellow-creatures. The gentle, mannerly sound of hand-clapping was a kind of light froth on the surface of the billowy sea of heartfelt applause. The host of the fifteen thousand might have just had their lives saved, or their children snatched from destruction and their wives from dishonour; they might have been preserved from bankruptcy, starvation, prison, torture; they might have been rewarding with their impassioned worship a band of national heroes. But it was not so. All that had happened was that the ball had rolled into the net of the Manchester Rovers' goal. Knype had drawn level. The reputation of the Five Towns before the jury of expert opinion that could distinguish between first-class football and second-class was maintained intact. I could hear specialists around me proving that though Knype had yet five League matches to play, its situation was safe. They pointed excitedly to a huge hoarding at one end of the ground on which appeared names of other clubs with changing figures. These clubs included the clubs which Knype would have to meet before the end of the season, and the figures indicated their fortunes on various grounds similar to this ground all over the country. If a goal was scored in Newcastle, or in Southampton, the very Peru of first-class football, it was registered on that board and its possible effect on the destinies of Knype was instantly assessed. The calculations made were dizzying.

Then a little flock of pigeons flew up and separated, under the illusion that they were free agents and masters of the air, but really wafted away to fixed destinations on the stupendous atmospheric waves of still-continued cheering.

After a minute or two the ball was restarted, and the greater noise had diminished to the sensitive uneasy murmur which responded like a delicate instrument to the fluctuations of the game. Each feat and manoeuvre of Knype drew generous applause in proportion to its intention or its success, and each sleight of the Manchester Rovers, successful or not, provoked a holy disgust. The attitude of the host had passed beyond morality into religion.

Then, again, while my attention had lapsed from the field, a devilish, a barbaric, and a deafening yell broke from those fifteen thousand passionate hearts. It thrilled me; it genuinely frightened me. I involuntarily made the motion of swallowing. After the thunderous crash of anger from the host came the thin sound of a whistle. The game stopped. I heard the same word repeated again and again, in divers tones of exasperated fury:

'Foul!'

I felt that I was hemmed in by potential homicides, whose arms were lifted in the desire of murder and whose features were changed from the likeness of man into the corporeal form of some pure and terrible instinct.

And I saw a long doll rise from the ground and approach a lesser doll with threatening hands.

'Foul! Foul!'

'Go it, Jos! Knock his neck out! Jos! He tripped thee up!'

There was a prolonged gesticulatory altercation between the three black dolls in leather leggings and several of the white and the red dolls. At last one of the mannikins in leggings shrugged his shoulders, made a definite gesture to the other two, and walked away towards the edge of the field nearest the stand. It was the unprincipled referee; he had disallowed the foul. In the protracted duel between the offending Manchester forward and the great, honest Jos Myatt he had given another point to the enemy. As soon as the host realized the infamy it yelled once more in heightened fury. It seemed to surge in masses against the thick iron railings that alone stood between the referee and death. The discreet referee was approaching the grand stand as the least unsafe place. In a second a handful of executioners had somehow got on to the grass. And in the next second several policemen were in front of them, not striking nor striving to intimidate, but heavily pushing them into bounds.

'Get back there!' cried a few abrupt, commanding voices from the stand.

The referee stood with his hands in his pockets and his whistle in his mouth. I think that in that moment of acutest suspense the whole of his earthly career must have flashed before him in a phantasmagoria. And then the crisis was past. The inherent gentle-manliness of the outraged host had triumphed and the referee was spared.

'Served him right if they'd man-handled him!' said a spectator.

'Ay!' said another, gloomily, 'ay! And th' Football Association 'ud ha' fined us maybe a hundred quid and disqualified th' ground for the rest o' th' season!'

'D – n th' Football Association!'

'Ay! But you canna'!'

'Now, lads! Play up, Knype! Now, lads! Give 'em hot hell!' Different voices heartily encouraged the home team as the ball was thrown into play.

The fouling Manchester forward immediately resumed posses-sion of the ball. Experience could not teach him. He parted with the ball and got it again, twice. The devil was in him and in the ball. The devil was driving him towards Myatt. They met. And then came a sound quite new: a cracking sound, somewhat like the snapping of a bough, but sharper, more decisive.

'By Jove!' exclaimed Stirling. 'That's his bone!'

ANONYMOUS

Curlers' Grace

O Lord wha's love surrounds us a'
   And brings us a' thegither;
Wha' writes your laws upon oor hearts,
   And bids us help each ither.
We bless Thee for Thy bounties great,
   For meat and hame and gear
We thank Thee, Lord, for snaw and ice –
   But still we ask for mair.
Gi'e us a hert to dae whit's richt,
   Like curlers true and keen;
To be guid friends along life's road,
   And soop oor slide aye clean.
O Power abune whose bounty free,
   Oor needs and wants suffices;
We render thanks for Barley Bree,
   And meat that appetises.
Be Thou our Skip throughout life's game,
   An' syne we're sure to win;
Tho' slow the shot and wide the aim,
   We'll soop each ither in.

6

THE CULTURE OF SPORT

There is a culture for sport as a whole and for each sport. For Leonard Gribble in The Arsenal Stadium Mystery the 'core of the soccer crowd', 'the hundred per cent fans', are those who stay behind after the game, those for whom the place and the time are as important as the match itself.

In William Basse's 'The Angler's Song', fishing is compared to hunting, tennis and courting. The poem talks about fishing for food, considers fish as symbols, and finishes with explicit moralising. The hunting references raise the question of whether fishing is sport. But the word 'sport' itself for most of the period of English literature has meant, primarily, hunting. Mentioned in the Wordsworth excerpt, hunting is also referenced in the passage from George Eliot's Daniel Deronda, where 'the time-honored British resource of 'killing something" has become sublimated into archery, or perhaps competing for position in society.

Dickens's portrayal of Derby Day at Epsom is about much more than horses galloping round a course; the race itself is dealt with in just one paragraph. Far more exciting is the being there, the picnics, the amusements, the clothes, the jugglers and fortune-tellers that swirl around the sport of kings. Hazlitt's obituary for the fives player John Cavanagh on the other hand turns inwards – the loss of a person 'who does any one thing better than any one else in the world' makes the world less.

Hazlitt makes a reference to 'Mr Wordsworth's epic poetry' as 'lumbering', but Wordsworth at his best is, like his subject, quick and 'sparkling clear'. Skating gives Wordsworth the opportunity to remember the delights of childhood company but also to turn aside, alone, to stand and watch.

CHARLES DICKENS

Epsom (1851)

On that great occasion, an unused spectator might imagine that all London turned out. There is little perceptible difference in the bustle of its crowded streets, but all the roads leading to Epsom Downs are so thronged and blocked by every description of carriage that it is marvellous to consider how, when, and where, they were all made – out of what possible wealth they are all maintained – and by what laws the supply of horses is kept equal to the demand. Near the favourite bridges, and at various leading points of the leading roads, clusters of people post themselves by nine o'clock, to see the Derby people pass. Then come flitting by barouches, phaetons, broughams, gigs, four-wheeled chaises, four-in-hands, Hansom cabs, cabs of lesser note, chaise-carts, donkey-carts, tilted vans made arborescent with green boughs and carrying no end of people, and a cask of beer – equestrians, pedestrians, horse-dealers, gentlemen, notabilities, and swindlers, by tens of thousands – gradually thickening and accumulating, until, at last, a mile short of the turnpike, they become wedged together, and are very slowly filtered through layers of policemen, mounted and a-foot, until, one by one, they pass the gate and skurry down the hill beyond. The most singular combinations occur in these turnpike stoppages and presses. Four-in-hand leaders look affectionately over the shoulders of ladies, in bright shawls, perched in gigs; poles of carriages appear, uninvited, in the midst of social parties in phaetons; little, fast, short-stepping ponies run up carriage-wheels before they can be stopped, and hold on behind like footmen. Now, the gentleman who is unaccustomed to public driving, gets into astonishing perplexities. Now, the Hansom cab whisks craftily in and out, and seems occasionally to fly over a waggon or so. Now the postboy on a jibbing or a shying horse curses the evil hour of his birth, and is ingloriously assisted by the shabby hostler out of place, who is walking down with seven shabby companions more or less equine, open to the various chances of the road. Now, the air is fresh, and the dust flies thick and fast. Now, the canvas-booths upon the course are seen to glisten and flutter in the distance. Now, the adventurous vehicles make cuts across, and get into ruts and gravel-pits. Now, the heather in bloom is like a field of gold, and the roar of voices is like a wind. Now, we leave the hard road and go smoothly rolling over the soft green turf, attended by an army of unfortunate worshippers in red jackets and stable-jackets, who make a very Juggernaut-car of our equipage, and now breathlessly call us 'My Lord,' and now, 'your Honour.' Now, we pass the outer settlements of tents where pots and kettles are – where gipsy children are – where airy stabling is – where tares for horses may be bought where water, water, water, is proclaimed – where the Tumbler in an old pea-coat, with a spangled fillet round his head, eats oysters, while his wife takes care of the golden globes, and the knives, and also of the starry little boy, their son, who lives principally upside-down. Now, we pay our one pound at the barrier, and go faster on, still Juggernaut-wise, attended by our devotees, until at last we are drawn, and rounded, and backed, and sidled, and cursed, and complimented, and vociferated into a station on the hill opposite the Grand Stand, where we presently find ourselves on foot, much bewildered, waited on by five respectful persons, who will brush us all at once.

Well, to be sure, there never was such a Derby Day, as this present Derby Day! Never, to be sure, were there so many carriages, so many fours, so many twos, so many ones, so many horsemen, so many people who have come down by 'rail,' so many fine ladies in so many broughams, so many of Fortnum and Mason's hampers, so much ice and champagne! If I were on the turf, and had a horse to enter for the Derby, I would call that horse Fortnum and Mason,

convinced that with that name he would beat the field. Public opinion would bring him in somehow. Look where I will – in some connexion with the carriages – made fast upon the top, or occupying the box, or tied up behind, or dangling below, or peeping out of window – I see Fortnum and Mason. And now, Heavens! All the hampers fly wide open, and the green Downs burst into a blossom of lobster-salad!

As if the great Trafalgar signal had been suddenly displayed from the top of the Grand Stand, every man proceeds to 'do his duty.' The weaker spirits, who were ashamed to set the great example, follow it instantly, and all around me there are table-cloths, pies, chickens, hams, tongues, rolls, lettuces, radishes, shell-fish, broad-bottomed bottles, clinking glasses, and carriages turned inside out. Amidst the hum of voices a bell rings. What's that? What's the matter? They are clearing the course. Never mind. Try the pigeon-pie. A roar. What's the matter? It's only the dog upon the course. Is that all? Glass of wine. Another roar. What's that? It's only the man who wants to cross the course, and is intercepted, and brought back. Is that all? I wonder whether it is always the same dog and the same man, year after year! A great roar. What's the matter? By Jupiter, they are going to start.

A deeper hum and a louder roar. Everybody standing on Fortnum and Mason. Now they're off'! No. *Now* they're off! No. *Now* they are off. No. *Now* they are! Yes!

There they go! Here they come! Where? Keep your eye on Tattenham Corner, and you'll see 'em coming round in half a minute. Good gracious, look at the Grand Stand, piled up with human beings to the top, and at the wonderful effect of changing light as all their faces and uncovered heads turn suddenly this way! Here they are! Who is? The horses! Where? Here they come! Green first. No: Red first. No: Blue first. No: the Favorite first. Who says so? Look! Hurrah! Hurrah! All over. Glorious race. Favourite wins! Two hundred thousand pounds lost and won. You don't say so? Pass the pie!

Now, the pigeons fly away with the news. Now, every one dismounts from the top of Fortnum and Mason, and falls to work with greater earnestness than before, on carriage boxes, sides, tops, wheels, steps, roofs, and rumbles. Now, the living stream upon the course, dammed for a little while at one point, is released, and spreads like parti-coloured grain. Now, the roof of the Grand Stand is deserted. Now, rings are formed upon the course, where strong men stand in pyramids on one another's heads; where the Highland lady dances; where the Devonshire Lad sets-to with the Bantam; where the Tumbler throws the golden globes about, with the starry little boy tied round him in a knot.

Now, all the variety of human riddles who propound themselves on race-courses, come about the carriages, to be guessed. Now, the gipsy woman, with the flashing red or yellow handkerchief about her head, and the strange silvery-hoarse voice, appears, 'My pretty gentleman, to tell your fortin, Sir; for you have a merry eye, my gentleman, and surprises is in store; for you're connected with a dark lady as loves you better than you love a kiss in a dark corner when the moon's a-shining; for you have a lively 'art, my gentleman, and you shall know her secret thoughts, and the first and last letters of her name, my pretty gentleman, if you will cross your poor gipsy's hand with a little bit of silver, for the luck of the fortin as the gipsy will read true, from the lines of your hand, my gentleman, both as to what is past, and present, and to come.' Now, the Ethiopians, looking unutterably hideous in the sunlight, play old banjoes and bones, on which no man could perform ten years ago, but which, it seems, any man may play now, if he will only blacken his face, put on a crisp wig, a white waistcoat and wristbands, a large white tie, and give his mind to it. Now, the sickly-looking ventriloquist, with an anxious face (and always with a wife in a shawl) teaches the alphabet to the puppet pupil, whom he takes out of his pocket. Now, my sporting gentlemen, you may ring the Bull, the Bull, the Bull; you may ring the Bull! Now, try your luck at the knock-em-downs, my Noble Swells – twelve heaves for sixpence, and a pincushion in the centre, worth ten times the money! Now the Noble Swells take five shillings' worth of 'heaves,' and carry off a halfpenny wooden pear in triumph. Now, it hails, as it always does hail, formidable wooden truncheons round the heads, bodies, and shins of the proprietors of the said knock-em-downs, whom nothing hurts. Now, inscrutable creatures, in smock frocks, beg for bottles. Now, a coarse vagabond, or idiot, or a compound of the two, never beheld by mortal off a race-course, hurries about, with ample skirts and a tattered parasol, counterfeiting a woman. Now, a shabby man, with an overhangmg forehead, and a slinking eye, produces a small board, and invites your attention to something novel and curious – three thimbles and one little pea – with a one, two, three – and a two, three, one – and a one – and a two – in the middle – right hand, left hand – go you any bet from a crown to five sovereigns you don't lift the thimble the pea's under! Now, another gentleman (with a stick) much interested in the experiment, will 'go' two sovereigns that he does lift the thimble, provided strictly that the shabby man holds his hand still, and don't touch 'em again. Now, the bet's made, and the gentleman with the stick lifts obviously the wrong thimble, and loses. Now, it is as clear as day to an innocent bystander, that the loser must have won if he had not blindly lifted the wrong thimble – in which he is strongly confirmed by another gentleman with a stick, also much interested, who proposes to 'go him' halves – a friendly sovereign to *his* sovereign against the bank. Now, the innocent agrees, and loses – and so the world turns round bringing innocents with it in abundance, though the three confederates are wretched actors, and could live by no other trade if they couldn't do it better.

LEONARD GRIBBLE

From *The Arsenal Stadium Mystery* (1939)

The dispersal of seventy thousand spectators is not achieved in a few minutes. At the top of Highbury Hill, foot and mounted police controlled the queues invading the Arsenal Station of the Underground. More mounted police kept the crowd in Avenell Road on the move. All the tributary roads were choked with cars that had been parked throughout the game. A score of taxi-drivers who had seen an opportunity of combining business with pleasure that afternoon now tried to worm their cabs through the throng, which took singularly small notice of honking horns and verbal exasperation. Peanut vendors and newsboys were exercising their lungs and taking steady flows of coppers for their trouble. Over the crowd hung a pall of tobacco smoke and dust.

'Come on now. Move along there.'

The good-humoured invitations of the police produced little apparent result. There is something viscous and sluggish about the mass movements of a football crowd that is homeward bound. Having witnessed a game it seemingly has one thought, to know the results of games played in every other corner of the Kingdom.

'Chelsea again – '

'See the Wolves got a netful.'

'What did the Wednesday do?'

'Another away win for Everton …'

'Got any Scottish results in your paper? How about the Rangers and Aberdeen?'

Pencils check the first batch of published results with pools forecasts. Anxious inquiries are answered with almost savage terseness.

'Draw…won away…lost at home …'

Slowly the bright possibility of those other match results fades, and interest returns to the game that has been watched. Fresh cigarettes are lit, more peanuts and chewing-gum are bought and munched, and discussion begins, sometimes heated, sometimes very partisan and not sincere, but never disinterested.

And all the time that shuffling, mooching crowd that has over-flowed on to every inch of pavement, gutter, and roadway is slowly pouring into Underground trains, buses, cars, and motor-coaches. There is plenty of shoving with elbows, trampling of less nimble feet, and poking of more prominent ribs. In the trains the corridors and entrance platforms are choked. Cigarettes are knocked from mouths and clothes are singed. Hands press heavily on strangers' shoulders.

'Sorry, mate.'

'That's all right, old man. We all got to get home, ain't we?'

The air is full of expunged breath, smoke, human smells, and heat. But there is plenty of laughter, plenty of Cockney chaff. Whatever happens, however great the discomfort, the crowd keeps its good-temper. This herded homegoing is just part of the after-noon's entertainment. The bigger the crowd the bigger the crush, and correspondingly the bigger the individual's satisfaction at being there.

'Record gate today, eh?'

'Must be.'

'Glad I didn't miss it.'

'Me too.'

That rib-bruising, foot-crushing scramble is endured with some-thing of pride. It is the final proof that the individual has not been wasting his time, that the game was worth seeing because every-body else wanted to see it. A generalization that holds strangely true throughout the entire soccer season.

Of course, there are the few who protest at the crush. But the real followers of football, the 'regulars', the 'supporters' who make the Leagues possible and provide Britain with a professional sport

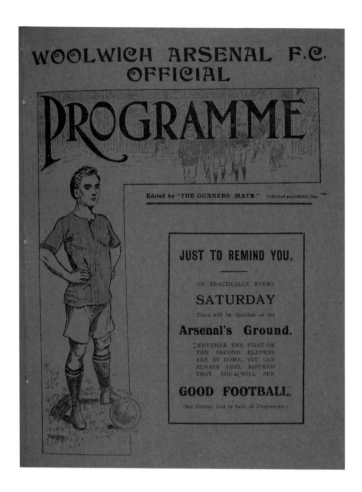

in which she is supreme, they have only tight-lipped contempt for the casual spectators – and occasionally a helpful suggestion.

But like every other natural tide, the football crowd leaves behind it tiny pools, groups who persist in debating some point of play on a street-corner, and of course at Highbury there is always that bigger pool that remains doggedly at the Stadium entrance.

These are the hundred per cent fans, the autograph-hunters, and the admirers of individual players. An hour, two hours after a game is over some of them are still there, unwearied, constant of mind and purpose.

These are the core of the soccer crowd, professional spectators, as it were. They follow 'their' team as a gull follows a ship, unswervingly, persistently. In the large window of present-day social entertainment they find a place with the professional first-nighters of the theatre and the professional clubmen of the West End, those Mayfair troglodytes who emerge into the open once every twenty-four hours, to see if the world still wags – outside the columns of *The Times*.

But while the crowd of seventy thousand take more than an hour to disperse, a much more animated scene occurs in the dressing rooms where the players relax.

Few of the Arsenal players, after that memorable match with the Trojans, noticed the worried look on Tom Whittaker's face when he joined them. As Whittaker took a cup of tea some one pushed into his hands, Eddie Hapgood was delivering himself as a veteran.

'They were as good as any First Division side we've met this season,' he averred.

WILLIAM BASSE

The Angler's Song (1653)

As inward love breeds outward talk,
The hound some praise, and some the hawk;
Some, better pleas'd with private sport
Use tennis, some a mistress court:
But these delights I neither wish
Nor envy, while I freely fish.

Who hunts, doth oft in danger ride,
Who hawks, lures oft both far and wide,
Who uses games shall often prove
A loser; but who falls in love,
Is fetter'd in fond Cupid's snare:
My angle breeds me no such care.

Of recreation there is none
So free as fishing is alone;
All other pastimes do no less
Than mind and body both possess;
My hand alone my work can do,
So I can fish and study too.

I care not, I, to fish in seas,
Fresh rivers best my mind do please,
Whose sweet calm course I contemplate,
And seek in life to imitate;
In civil bounds I fain would keep,
And for my past offences weep.

And when the timorous trout I wait
To take, and he devours my bait,
How poor a thing, sometimes I find,
Will captivate a greedy mind;
And when none bite, I praise the wise
Whom vain allurements ne'er surprise.

But yet, though while I fish I fast,
I make good fortune my repast;
And hereunto my friend invite,
In whom I more then that delight:
Who is more welcome to my dish,
Than to my angle was my fish.

As well content no prize to take,
As use of taken prize to make;
For so our Lord was pleased, when
He fishers made fishers of men;
Where, which is in no other game,
A man may fish and praise his name.

The first men that our Saviour dear
Did choose to wait upon him here,
Blest fishers were; and fish the last
Food was that he on earth did taste;
I therefore strive to follow those
Whom he to follow him hath chose.

GEORGE ELIOT

From *Daniel Deronda* (1876)

Who can deny that bows and arrows are among the prettiest weapons in the world for feminine forms to play with? They prompt attitudes full of grace and power, where that fine concentration of energy seen in all markmanship is freed from associations of blood-shed. The time-honored British resource of 'killing something' is no longer carried on with bow and quiver; bands defending their passes against an invading nation fight under another sort of shade than a cloud of arrows; and poisoned darts are harmless survivals either in rhetoric or in regions comfortably remote. Archery has no ugly smell of brimstone; breaks nobody's shins, breeds no athletic monsters; its only danger is that of failing, which for generous blood is enough to mould skilful action. And among the Brackenshaw archers the prizes were all of the nobler symbolic kind; not properly to be carried off in a parcel, degrading honour into gain; but the gold arrow and the silver, the gold star and the silver, to be worn for a long time in sign of achievement and then transferred to the next who did excellently. These signs of pre-eminence had the virtue of wreaths without their inconveniences, which might have produced a melancholy effect in the heat of the ball-room. Altogether the Brackenshaw Archery Club was an institution framed with good taste, so as not to have by necessity any ridiculous incidents.

And today all incalculable elements were in its favour. There was mild warmth, and no wind to disturb either hair or drapery or the course of the arrow; all skillful preparation had fair play, and when there was a general march to extract the arrows, the prom-enade of joyous young creatures in light speech and laughter, the graceful movement in common toward a common object, was a show worth looking at. Here Gwendolen seemed a Calypso among

her nymphs. It was in her attitudes and movements that every one was obliged to admit her surpassing charm.

'That girl is like a high-mettled racer,' said Lord Brackenshaw to young Clintock, one of the invited spectators.

'First chop! Tremendously pretty too,' said the elegant Grecian, who had been paying her assiduous attention; 'I never saw her look better.'

Perhaps she had never looked so well. Her face was beaming with young pleasure in which there was no malign rays of discontent; for being satisfied with her own chances, she felt kindly toward everybody and was satisfied with the universe. Not to have the highest distinction in rank, not to be marked out as an heiress, like Miss Arrowpoint, gave an added triumph in eclipsing those advantages. For personal recommendation she would not have cared to change the family group accompanying her for any other: her mamma's appearance would have suited an amiable duchess; her uncle and aunt Gascoigne with Anna made equally gratifying figures in their way; and Gwendolen was too full of joyous belief in herself to feel in the least jealous, though Miss Arrowpoint was one of the best archeresses.

WILLIAM HAZLITT

The Indian Jugglers (1828)

'Died at his house in Burbage Street, St Giles's, John Cavanagh, the
famous hand fives-player.' When a person dies who does any one
thing better than any one else in the world, which so many others
are trying to do well, it leaves a gap in society. It is not likely that any
one will now see the game of fives played in its perfection for many
years to come – for Cavanagh is dead, and has not left his peer
behind him. It may be said that there are things of more importance than striking a ball against a wall – there are things, indeed,
that make more noise and do as little good, such as making war and
peace, making speeches and answering them, making verses and
blotting them, making money and throwing it away. But the game
of fives is what no one despises who has ever played at it. It is the
finest exercise for the body, and the best relaxation for the mind.
The Roman poet said that 'Care mounted behind the horseman
and stuck to his skirts.' But this remark would not have applied
to the fives-player. He who takes to playing at fives is twice young.
He feels neither the past nor future 'in the instant.' Debts, taxes,
'domestic treason, foreign levy, nothing can touch him further.' He
has no other wish, no other thought, from the moment the game
begins, but that of striking the ball, of placing it, of making it! This
Cavanagh was sure to do. Whenever he touched the ball there was
an end of the chase. His eye was certain, his hand fatal, his presence
of mind complete. He could do what he pleased, and he always
knew exactly what to do. He saw the whole game, and played it; took
instant advantage of his adversary's weakness, and recovered balls,
as if by a miracle and from sudden thought, that every one gave
for lost. He had equal power and skill, quickness and judgment. He
could either outwit his antagonist by finesse, or beat him by main

strength. Sometimes, when he seemed preparing to send the ball with the full swing of his arm, he would by a slight turn of his wrist drop it within an inch of the line. In general, the ball came from his hand, as if from a racket, in a straight, horizontal line; so that it was in vain to attempt to overtake or stop it. As it was said of a great orator that he never was at a loss for a word, and for the properest word, so Cavanagh always could tell the degree of force necessary to be given to a ball, and the precise direction in which it should be sent. He did his work with the greatest ease; never took more pains than was necessary; and while others were fagging themselves to death, was as cool and collected as if he had just entered the court. His style of play was as remarkable as his power of execution. He had no affectation, no trifling. He did not throw away the game to show off an attitude or try an experiment. He was a fine, sensible, manly player, who did what he could, but that was more than any one else could even affect to do. His blows were not undecided and ineffectual – lumbering like Mr Wordsworth's epic poetry, nor wavering like Mr Coleridge's lyric prose, nor short of the mark like Mr Brougham's speeches, nor wide of it like Mr Canning's wit, nor foul like the Quarterly, nor let balls like the *Edinburgh Review.* Cobbett and Junius together would have made a Cavanagh. He was the best up-hill player in the world; even when his adversary was fourteen, he would play on the same or better, and as he never flung away the game through carelessness and conceit, he never gave it through laziness or want of heart. The only peculiarity of his play was that he never volleyed, but let the balls hop; but if they rose an inch from the ground he never missed having them. There was not only nobody equal, but nobody second to him. It is supposed that he could give any other player half the game, or beat him with his left hand. His service was tremendous. He once played Woodward and Meredith together (two of the best players in England) in the Fives-court, St Martin's street, and made seven and twenty aces following by services alone – a thing unheard of. He another time played Peru, who was considered a first-rate fives-player, a match of the best out of five games, and in the three first games, which of course decided the match, Peru got only one ace. Cavanagh was an Irishman by birth, and a house-painter by profession. He had once laid aside his working-dress, and walked up, in his smartest clothes, to the Rosemary Branch to have an afternoon's pleasure. A person accosted him, and asked him if he would have a game. So they agreed to play for half a crown a game and a bottle of cider. The first game began – it was seven, eight, ten, thirteen, fourteen, all. Cavanagh won it. The next was the same. They played on, and each game was hardly contested. 'There,' said the unconscious fives-player, 'there was a stroke that Cavanagh could not take: I never played better in my life, and yet I can't win a game. I don't know how it is!' However, they played on, Cavanagh winning every game, and the bystanders drinking the cider and laughing all the time. In the twelfth game, when Cavanagh was only four, and the stranger thirteen, a person came in and said, 'What! Are you here, Cavanagh?' The words were no sooner pronounced than the astonished player let the ball drop from his hand, and saying, 'What! Have I been breaking my heart all this time to beat Cavanagh?' refused to make another effort. 'And yet, I give you my word,' said Cavanagh, telling the story with some triumph, 'I played all the while with my clenched fist.'

WILLIAM WORDSWORTH

From *The Prelude* (1888)

And in the frosty season, when the sun
Was set, and visible for many a mile
The cottage windows blazed through twilight gloom,
I heeded not their summons: happy time
It was indeed for all of us – for me
It was a time of rapture! Clear and loud
The village clock tolled six – I wheeled about,
Proud and exulting like an untired horse
That cares not for his home. All shod with steel,
We hissed along the polished ice in games
Confederate, imitative of the chase
And woodland pleasures – the resounding horn,
The pack loud chiming, and the hunted hare.
So through the darkness and the cold we flew,
And not a voice was idle; with the din
Smitten, the precipices rang aloud;
The leafless trees and every icy crag
Tinkled like iron; while far distant hills
Into the tumult sent an alien sound
Of melancholy not unnoticed, while the stars
Eastward were sparkling clear, and in the west
The orange sky of evening died away.
Not seldom from the uproar I retired
Into a silent bay, or sportively
Glanced sideway, leaving the tumultuous throng,
To cut across the reflex of a star
That fled, and, flying still before me, gleamed
Upon the glassy plain; and oftentimes,

When we had given our bodies to the wind,
And all the shadowy banks on either side
Came sweeping through the darkness, spinning still
The rapid line of motion, then at once
Have I, reclining back upon my heels,
Stopped short; yet still the solitary cliffs
Wheeled by me – even as if the earth had rolled
With visible motion her diurnal round!
Behind me did they stretch in solemn train,
Feebler and feebler, and I stood and watched
Till all was tranquil as a dreamless sleep.

Ye Presences of Nature in the sky
And on the earth! Ye Visions of the hills!
And Souls of lonely places! Can I think
A vulgar hope was yours when ye employed
Such ministry, when ye, through many a year
Haunting me thus among my boyish sports,
On caves and trees, upon the woods and hills,
Impressed, upon all forms, the characters
Of danger or desire; and thus did make
The surface of the universal earth,
With triumph and delight, with hope and fear,
Work like a sea?

7

LOVE AND HATE

The four final texts take us to a different place, beyond the euphoria of success and the despair of failure. They explore the point where opposites meet and where the opponent is both enemy and friend. Hemingway's boy, David – and I suggest there is no coincidence in that name – comes to love the fish which not only survives his attempt to catch it but leaves him with nothing; Birkin and Gerald understand that fighting allows them a closeness that is unachievable in any other manner. The memory of the ultimate experience of defeat – the death of friends – sharpens Whymper's appreciation of the life-enhancing nature of mountaineering.

Joyce Carol Oates came to boxing as a child, and her On Boxing has been celebrated as some of the most penetrating writing on the subject, combining ringside knowledge with an acute awareness of the frightening complicity of the spectator. Though she is aware of the metaphorical potential of boxing, she suggests that we should not think of boxing as a metaphor for life. 'Life is like boxing in many unsettling respects. But boxing is only like boxing.'

So is sport like life, or is life like sport? This doubt is applicable to all four of the situations in these final passages. Birkin and Gerald become one through their physical struggle against each other, just as David and the fighting fish are brought together. Whymper's personal struggle against altitude brings him closer to himself and to other people. Sport is a means to an end, but an end which can be achieved only through this particular activity – it is both ancillary and essential. This bewildering, ugly and beautiful jamming together of opposites is what Oates gives us, in what is, for me, some of the best writing, not just on boxing, but on this whole business of testing our bodies and our wills as far as they can go.

ERNEST HEMINGWAY

From *Islands in the Stream* (1970)

'Fish!' Thomas Hudson heard young Tom shout. 'Fish! Fish! There he comes up. Behind you, Dave. Watch him!'

Thomas Hudson saw a huge boil in the water but could not see the fish. David had the rod butt in the gimble and was looking up at the clothespin on the outrigger in a long, slow loop that tightened as it hit the water and now was racing out at a slant, slicing the water as it went.

'Hit him, Dave. Hit him hard,' Eddy called from the companionway.

'Hit him, Dave. For God's sake hit him,' Andrew begged.

'Shut up,' David said. 'I'm handling him.'

He hadn't struck yet and the line was steadily going out at the angle, the rod bowed, the boy holding back on it as the line moved out. Thomas Hudson throttled the motors down so they were barely turning over.

'Oh for God's sake, hit him,' Andrew pleaded. 'Or let me hit him.'

David just held back on the rod and watched the line moving out at the same steady angle. He had loosened the drag.

'He's a broadbill, papa,' he said without looking up. 'I saw his sword when he took it.'

'Honest to God?' Andrew asked. 'Oh boy.'

'I think you ought to hit him now,' Roger was standing with the boy now. He had the back out of the chair and he was buckling the harness on the reel. 'Hit him now, Dave, and really hit him.'

'Do you think he's had it long enough?' David asked. 'You don't think he's had it long enough?' David asked. 'You don't think he's just carrying it in his mouth and swimming with it?'

'I think you better hit him before he spits it out.'

David braced his feet, tightened the drag well down with his right hand, and struck back hard against the great weight. He struck again and again bending the rod like a bow. The line moved out steadily. He had made no impression on the fish.

'Hit him again, Dave,' Roger said. 'Really put it into him.'

David struck again with all his strength and the line started zizzing out, the rod bent so that he could hardly hold it.

'Oh God,' he said devoutly. 'I think I've got it into him.'

'Ease up on your drag,' Roger told him. 'Turn with him, Tom, and watch the line.'

'Turn with him and watch the line,' Thomas Hudson repeated. 'You all right, Dave?'

'I'm wonderful, papa,' Dave said. 'Oh God, if I can catch this fish.'

Thomas Hudson swung the boat around almost on her stern. Dave's line was fading off the reel and Thomas Hudson moved up on the fish.

'Tighten up and get that line in now,' Roger said. 'Work on him, Dave.'

David was lifting and reeling as he lowered, lifting and reeling as he lowered, as regularly as a machine, and was getting back a good quantity of line on to his reel.

'Nobody in our family's ever caught a broadbill,' Andrew said.

'Oh keep your mouth off him, please,' David said. 'Don't put your mouth on him.'

'Do you think his mouth will hold?' young Tom whispered to his father, who was holding the wheel and looking down into the stern and watching the slant of the white line in the dark water.

'I hope so. Dave isn't strong enough to be rough with him.'

'I'll do anything if we can get him,' young Tom said. 'Anything. I'll give up anything. I'll promise anything. Get him some water, Andy.'

'I've got some,' Eddy said. 'Stay with him, old Dave boy.'

'I don't want him any closer,' Roger called up. He was a great fisherman, and he and Thomas Hudson understood each other perfectly in a boat.

'I'll put him astern,' Thomas Hudson called and swung the boat around very softly and easily so the stern hardly disturbed the calm sea.

The fish was sounding now and Thomas Hudson backed the boat very slowly to ease the pressure on the line all that he could. But with only a touch of reverse with the stern moving slowly towards the fish the angle was all gone from the line and the rod tip was pointing straight down and the line kept going out in a series of steady jerks, the rod bucking each time in David's hands. Thomas Hudson slipped the boat ahead just a touch so that the boy would not have the line so straight up and down in the water. He knew how it was pulling on his back in that position, but he had to save all the line he could.

'I can't put any more drag on or it will break,' David said. 'What will he do, Mr Davis?'

'He'll just keep on going down until you stop him,' Roger said. 'Or until he stops. Then you've got to try to get him up.'

The line kept going out and down, out and down, out and down. The rod was bent so far it looked as though it must break and the line was taut as a tuned cello string and there was not much more of it on the reel.

'What can I do, papa?'

'Nothing. You're doing what there is to do.'

EDWARD WHYMPER

From *Scrambles Amongst the Alps in the Years 1860–69* (1871)

We who go mountain-scrambling have constantly set before us the superiority of fixed purpose or perseverance to brute force. We know that each height, each step, must be gained by patient, laborious toil, and that wishing cannot take the place of working: we know the benefits of mutual aid; that many a difficulty must be encountered, and many an obstacle must be grappled with or turned; but we know that where there's a will there's a way; and we come back to our daily occupations better fitted to fight the battle of life and to overcome the impediments which obstruct our paths, strengthened and cheered by the recollection of past labours, and by the memories of victories gained in other fields.

I have not made myself an advocate or an apologist for mountaineering, nor do I now intend to usurp the functions of a moralist; but my task would have been ill performed if it had been concluded without one reference to the more serious lessons of the mountaineer. We glory in the physical regeneration which is the product of our exertions; we exult over the grandeur of the scenes that are brought before our eyes, the splendours of sunrise and sunset, and the beauties of hill, dale, lake, wood and waterfall; but we value more highly the development of manliness, and the evolution, under combat with difficulties, of those noble qualities of human nature – courage, patience, endurance and fortitude.

Some hold these virtues in less estimation, and assign base and contemptible motives to those who indulge in our innocent sport. 'Be thou chaste as ice, as pure as snow, thou shalt not escape calumny.'

Others, again, who are not detractors, find mountaineering, as

a sport, to be wholly unintelligible. It is not greatly to be wondered at – we are not all constituted alike. Mountaineering is a pursuit essentially adapted to the young or vigorous, and not to the old or feeble. To the latter toil may be no pleasure; and it is often said by such persons, 'This man is making a toil of pleasure.' Toil he must who goes mountaineering, but out of the toil comes strength (not merely muscular energy – more than that), an awakening of all the faculties; and from the strength arises pleasure. Then, again, it is often asked, in tones which seem to imply that the answer must at least be doubtful, 'But does it repay you?' Well, we cannot estimate our enjoyment as you measure your wine or weigh your lead – it is real, nevertheless. If I could blot out every reminiscence or erase every memory, still I should say that my scrambles amongst the

Alps have repaid me, for they have given me two of the best things a man can possess – health and friends.

The recollections of past pleasures cannot be effaced. Even now as I write they crowd up before me. First comes an endless series of pictures, magnificent in form, effect and colour. I see the great peaks with clouded tops, seeming to mount up for ever and ever; I hear the music of the distant herds, the peasant's *jodel* and the solemn church-bells; and I scent the fragrant breath of the pines; and after these have passed away another train of thoughts succeeds – of those who have been upright, brave and true; of kind hearts and bold deeds; and of courtesies received at stranger hands, trifles in themselves, but expressive of that good will toward men which is the essence of charity.

Still, the last sad memory hovers round, and sometimes drifts across like floating mist, cutting off sunshine and chilling the remembrance of happier times. There have been joys too great to be described in words, and there have been griefs upon which I have not dared to dwell; and with these in mind I say climb if you will, but remember that courage and strength are naught without prudence, and that a momentary negligence may destroy the happiness of a lifetime. Do nothing in haste; look well to each step; and from the beginning think what may be the end.

D. H. LAWRENCE

From *Women in Love* (1920)

Gerald fastened the door and pushed the furniture aside. The room was large, there was plenty of space, it was thickly carpeted. Then he quickly threw off his clothes, and waited for Birkin. The latter, white and thin, came over to him. Birkin was more a presence than a visible object, Gerald was aware of him completely, but not really visually. Whereas Gerald himself was concrete and noticeable, a piece of pure final substance.

'Now,' said Birkin, 'I will show you what I learned, and what I remember. You let me take you so – ' And his hands closed on the naked body of the other man. In another moment, he had Gerald swung over lightly and balanced against his knee, head downwards. Relaxed, Gerald sprang to his feet with eyes glittering.

'That's smart,' he said. 'Now try again.'

So the two men began to struggle together. They were very dissimilar. Birkin was tall and narrow, his bones were very thin and fine. Gerald was much heavier and more plastic. His bones were strong and round, his limbs were rounded, all his contours were beautifully and fully moulded. He seemed to stand with a proper, rich weight on the face of the earth, whilst Birkin seemed to have the centre of gravitation in his own middle. And Gerald had a rich, frictional kind of strength, rather mechanical, but sudden and invincible, whereas Birkin was abstract as to be almost intangible. He impinged invisibly upon the other man, scarcely seeming to touch him, like a garment, and then suddenly piercing in a tense fine grip that seemed to penetrate into the very quick of Gerald's being.

They stopped, they discussed methods, they practised grips and throws, they became accustomed to each other, to each other's rhythm, they got a kind of mutual physical understanding. And

then again they had a real struggle. They seemed to drive their white flesh deeper and deeper against each other, as if they would break into a oneness. Birkin had a great subtle energy, that would press upon the other man with an uncanny force, weigh him like a spell put upon him. Then it would pass, and Gerald would heave free, with white, heaving, dazzling movements.

So the two men entwined and wrestled with each other, working nearer and nearer. Both were white and clear, but Gerald flushed smart red where he was touched, and Birkin remained white and tense. He seemed to penetrate into Gerald's more solid, more diffuse bulk, to interfuse his body through the body of the other, as if to bring it subtly into subjection, always seizing with some rapid necromantic fore-knowledge every motion of the other flesh, converting and counteracting it, playing upon the limbs and trunk of Gerald like some hard wind. It was as if Birkin's whole physical

intelligence interpenetrated into Gerald's body, as if his fine, sublimated energy entered into the flesh of the fuller man, like some
potency, casting a fine net, a prison, through the muscles into the
very depths of Gerald's physical being.

So they wrestled swiftly, rapturously, intent and mindless at last,
two essential white figures working into a tighter closer oneness
of struggle, with a strange, octopus-like knotting and flashing of
limbs in the subdued light of the room; a tense white knot of flesh
gripped in silence between the walls of old brown books. Now and
again came a sharp gasp of breath, or a sound like a sigh, then the
rapid thudding of movement on the thickly carpeted floor, then
the strange sound of flesh escaping under flesh. Often, in the white
interlaced knot of violent living being that swayed silently, there was
no head to be seen, only the swift, tight limbs, the solid white backs,
the physical junction of two bodies clinched into oneness. Then
would appear the gleaming, ruffled head of Gerald, as the struggle
changed, then for a moment the dun-coloured, shadow-like head
of the other man would lift up from the conflict, the eyes wide and
dreadful and sightless.

At length Gerald lay back inert on the carpet, his breast rising in
great slow panting, whilst Birkin kneeled over him, almost unconscious. Birkin was much more exhausted. He caught little, short
breaths, he could scarcely breathe any more. The earth seemed to
tilt and sway, and a complete darkness was coming over his mind.
He did not know what happened. He slid forward quite unconscious, over Gerald, and Gerald did not notice. Then he was
half-conscious again, aware only of the strange tilting and sliding
of the world. The world was sliding, everything was sliding off into
the darkness. And he was sliding, endlessly, endlessly away.

He came to consciousness again, hearing an immense knocking
outside. What could be happening, what was it, the great hammer-
stroke resounding through the house? He did not know. And then
it came to him that it was his own heart beating. But that seemed

impossible, the noise was outside. No, it was inside himself, it was his own heart. And the beating was painful, so strained, surcharged. He wondered if Gerald heard it. He did not know whether he were standing or lying or falling.

When he realised that he had fallen prostrate upon Gerald's body he wondered, he was surprised. But he sat up, steadying himself with his hand and waiting for his heart to become stiller and less painful. It hurt very much, and took away his consciousness.

Gerald however was still less conscious than Birkin. They waited dimly, in a sort of not-being, for many uncounted, unknown minutes.

'Of course – ' panted Gerald, 'I didn't have to be rough – with you – I had to keep back – my force – '

Birkin heard the sound as if his own spirit stood behind him, outside him, and listened to it. His body was in a trance of exhaustion, his spirit heard thinly. His body could not answer. Only he knew his heart was getting quieter. He was divided entirely between his spirit, which stood outside, and knew, and his body, that was a plunging, unconscious stroke of blood.

'I could have thrown you – using violence – ' panted Gerald. 'But you beat me right enough.'

'Yes,' said Birkin, hardening his throat and producing the words in the tension there, 'you're much stronger than I – you could beat me – easily.'

Then he relaxed again to the terrible plunging of his heart and his blood.

'It surprised me,' panted Gerald, 'what strength you've got. Almost supernatural.'

'For a moment,' said Birkin.

He still heard as if it were his own disembodied spirit hearing, standing at some distance behind him. It drew nearer however, his spirit. And the violent striking of blood in his chest was sinking quieter, allowing his mind to come back. He realised that he was leaning with all his weight on the soft body of the other man. It startled him, because he thought he had withdrawn. He recovered himself, and sat up. But he was still vague and unestablished. He put out his hand to steady himself. It touched the hand of Gerald, that was lying out on the floor. And Gerald's hand closed warm and sudden over Birkin's, they remained exhausted and breathless, the one hand clasped closely over the other. It was Birkin whose hand, in swift response, had closed in a strong, warm clasp over the hand of the other. Gerald's clasp had been sudden and momentaneous.

The normal consciousness however was returning, ebbing back. Birkin could breathe almost naturally again. Gerald's hand slowly withdrew, Birkin slowly, dazedly rose to his feet and went towards the table. He poured out a whiskey and soda. Gerald also came for a drink.

'It was a real set-to, wasn't it?' said Birkin, looking at Gerald with darkened eyes.

'God, yes,' said Gerald. He looked at the delicate body of the other man, and added: 'It wasn't too much for you, was it?'

'No. One ought to wrestle and strive and be physically close. It makes one sane.'

'You do think so?'

'I do. Don't you?'

'Yes,' said Gerald.

JOYCE CAROL OATES

From *On Boxing* (1987)

To the untrained eye most boxing matches appear not merely savage but mad. As the eye becomes trained, however, the spectator begins to see the complex patterns that underlie the 'madness'; what seems to be merely confusing action is understood to be coherent and intelligent, frequently inspired. Even the spectator who dislikes violence in principle can come to admire highly skillful boxing – to admire it beyond all 'sane' proportions. A brilliant boxing match, quicksilver in its motions, transpiring far more rapidly than the mind can absorb, can have the power that Emily Dickinson attributed to great poetry: you know it's great when it takes the top of your head off. (The physical imagery Dickinson employs is peculiarly apt in this context.)

This early impression – that boxing is 'mad,' or mimics the actions of madness – seems to me no less valid, however, for being, by degrees, substantially modified. It is never erased, never entirely forgotten or overcome; it simply sinks beneath the threshold of consciousness, as the most terrifying and heartrending of our lives' experiences sink beneath the level of consciousness by way of familiarity or deliberate suppression. So one knows, but does not (consciously) know, certain intransigent facts about the human condition. One does not (consciously) know, but one *knows*. All boxing fans, however accustomed to the sport, however many decades have been invested in their obsession, know that boxing is sheerly madness, for all its occasional beauty. That knowledge is our common bond and sometimes – dare it be uttered? – our common shame.

To watch boxing closely, and seriously, is to risk moments of what might be called animal panic – a sense not only that something very ugly is happening but that, by watching it, one is an accomplice. This awareness, or revelation, or weakness, or hairline split in one's cuticle of a self can come at any instant, unanticipated and unbidden; though of course it tends to sweep over the viewer when he is watching a really violent match. I feel it as vertigo – breathlessness – a repugnance beyond language: a sheerly physical loathing. That it is also, or even primarily, self-loathing goes without saying.

For boxing really isn't metaphor, it is the thing in itself. And my predilection for watching matches on tape, when the outcomes are known, doesn't alter the fact that, as the matches occurred, they occurred in the present tense, and for one time only. The rest is subterfuge – the intellectual's uneasy 'control' of his material.

For one friend of mine it was a bloody fight fought by the lightweight contender Bobby Chacon that filled him with horror – though, ironically, Chacon came back to win the match (as Chacon was once apt to do). For another friend, a fellow novelist, enamoured of boxing since boyhood, it was the Hagler-Hearns fight of 1985 – he was frightened by his own ecstatic participation in it.

At such times one thinks: What is happening? Why are we here? What does this mean? Can't this be stopped? My terror at seeing Floyd Patterson battered into insensibility by Sonny Liston was not assuaged by my rational understanding that the event had taken place long ago and that, in fact, Patterson is in fine health at the present time, training an adopted son to box. (Liston of course has been dead for years – he died of a heroin overdose, aged thirty-eight, in 'suspicious' circumstances.) More justified, perhaps, was my sickened sense that boxing is, simply, wrong, a mistake, an outlaw activity for some reason under the protectorate of the law, when, a few weeks ago in March 1986, I sat in the midst of a suddenly very quiet closed-circuit television audience in a suburban Trenton hall watching bantamweight Richie Sandoval as he lay flat and unmoving on his back … very likely dead of a savage beating the referee had not, for some reason, stopped in time. My conviction was that anything was preferable to boxing, anything was preferable to seeing another minute of it, for instance standing outside in the parking lot for the remainder of the evening and staring at the stained asphalt …

A friend who is a sportswriter was horrified by the same fight. In a letter he spoke of his intermittent disgust for the sport he has been watching most of his life, and writing about for years: 'It's all a bit like bad love – putting up with the pain, waiting for the sequel to the last good moment. And like bad love, there comes the point of being worn out, when the reward of the good moment doesn't seem worth all the trouble …'

Yet we don't give up on boxing, it isn't that easy. Perhaps it's like tasting blood. Or, more discreetly put, love commingled with hate is more powerful than love. Or hate.

LIST OF ILLUSTRATIONS

p. 68 *Golf Illustrated* 20/3/1925, p. 303 detail.

p. 77 Polo in the Afternoon, from *Harper's Weekly*, volume 1895, p. 422 (LOU.A.107).

p. 83 Cross at Polo. Drawn by John Charlton from a sketch by Major H.W. Helyar, *Harper's Weekly*, volume 1895, p. 165 (LOU.A.107).

p. 90 Leander swimming the Hellespont. Print by Cornelis Bloemaert after Abraham van Diepenbeeck, *c.* 1635–38, British Museum, 1973 (0616.43).

p. 95 'How the Fight was Won', drawn by Septimus E. Scott, from *Illustrated Sporting and Dramatic News* 25/07/1914, p. 953.

p. 98 Poster for Stockholm Olympics, 1912. Gustaf Gustafsson Uggla, Olympiska spelen i Stockholm 1912, 1912 (7906.h.28).

p. 102 'Avarice: Atalanta stopping to pick the golden apples up, while Hippomenes keeps running'. Etching and engraving by Edme Jeurat, 1713. British Museum, 1891 (1013.78).

p. 110 The Finish of the Derby, 1914, from *Illustrated Sporting and Dramatic News* 20/06/1914, pp. 708–709.

p. 121 Prize Fight, from Henry Thomas Alken, *The National Sports of Great Britain*, 1821, plate before f.38 (1818.c.6).

p. 127 Thomas Cribb, frontispiece from *Pierce Egan, Boxiana: or, Sketches of Ancient and Modern Pugilism, 1818–24*, (2270.e.8.(1)).

p. 130 W. W. Denslow, *When I Grow Up*, 1909, p. 89 (12804.y.21).

p. 141 Oxford v. Cambridge – A Run, from *Illustrated Sporting and Dramatic News* 19/12/1896, p. 617.

p. 158 A group of figures fishing by a river. Pen and brown ink, with watercolour. Anonymous Venetian artist, 18th C. British Museum, 1901 (0417.22).

p. 167 'The Art of Fencing or The Sword and Dagger Guard; two men fencing, swords in their left and daggers in their right hands, he on the left, parrying with his dagger his opponent's sword in tierce, with a wig on the ground'. Brush drawing in brown wash, over graphite, drawn by Marcellos Laroon II, 1648–1701, from *The Art of Fencing, c.* 1750 (C.141.aa.3, pl.1-2).

p. 169 Study of a man seated, fishing; wearing a cloak and broad-rimmed hat, sitting by a river in profile to left, the river bending into the distance Black chalk with grey and yellow wash. Drawn by Aelbert Cuyp, 1635–1691, British Museum, 1895 (0915.1143)

p. 171 William Blake, *Songs of Innocence and of Experience*, 1923, p.6 (C.71.d.19)

First published in 2016 by
The British Library
96 Euston Road
London NW1 2DT

Cataloguing in Publication Data
A catalogue record for this publication is available
from The British Library

ISBN 978 0 7123 0973 8

Introductions © Julian Walker 2016
Text compilation and editorial © Julian Walker 2016

Designed and typeset by Briony Hartley, Goldust Design
Picture research by Sally Nicholls
Printed in Malta by Gutenberg Press

CREDITS